Heavenly Tails

Heartwarming Stories of a Pet's Love

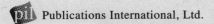 Publications International, Ltd.

Contributing Writers: Suzanne Jordan Browne, Sonia Weiss Castleberry, Elaine Creasman, Joe Curreri, Heather Down, Susan Farr Fahncke, Mary Fons-Misetic, Jackie Hirtz, Marie D. Jones, Kayla Kirkland, Karen McCarraher, Carol Stigger, Mildred W. Stinson, Sue Sveum, Jen Wesh, Lou Killian Zywicki

Cover Photo: shutterstock.com

Interior Illustrations: shutterstock.com

ISBN-13: 978-1-4508-7100-6
ISBN-10: 1-4508-7100-3

Manufactured in USA.

8 7 6 5 4 3 2 1

Contents

Endless Love

A pet's love is endless, and its devotion is limitless. Pets comfort us when we need it most, bring smiles to our faces when we require some cheering up, and rarely expect much in return except a little love and care.

The human-animal bond has long been a strong one. Dogs, cats, and creatures often take on the role of friend, teacher, parent, and partner. They adore us, heal us, and make us laugh. They teach us about enduring devotion, mend our hearts through breakups, and often break our hearts when they are no longer here. We may rescue them from a shelter or the street, but the truth is, they rescue us.

The stories here are testaments to this. In each tale, we can find an example of an animal's love. Some pets express a love that is neither loud nor showy, like something as straightforward as sitting next to us on the couch or wagging their tails when we get home. Some pets exhibit a loyalty that would even label them heroes.

A pet's devotion has no bounds. No matter what our situation, a pet's love has the power to inspire us all.

Made for Each Other

Snoopy, a little gray schnauzer, sat curled up in Harry's lap as though he belonged there. And he did. An unusual path had brought these two together, but it's certainly obvious to those who see them that they were made for each other.

Harry always joked that kids, dogs, and old ladies loved him, but he had never actually owned a dog of his own. He adored his daughter's golden retriever, Gus, who always came running the minute Harry walked through the door. But just like his grandchildren, Harry considered the dog a delight to visit but not to take home permanently. Harry liked Butch, the neighbor's dog, and Leah, the therapy dog that visited the assisted-living home where he volunteered. But at 87 years old, it never occurred to Harry that his canine-free life was about to change.

The real adjustment period started when Harry lost his wife of 64 years to cancer. The two were inseparable, especially after Harry retired, and her passing upended his life. Harry often visited the kids and grandkids and added more hours of volunteer work to fill his lonely days, but it wasn't enough.

One day while petting Leah at the assisted-living home, Sara, the therapy dog's owner, commented that the dog seemed especially drawn to him. It was the "kids and dogs syndrome," Harry explained, but she thought it might be more than that. Sara told him about a program at the local shelter that matched seniors with senior pets, but Harry just laughed. "It's not for me," he said.

Weeks passed, and Harry was getting through the days, albeit not easily. He was still very sad, feeling as though his life would never be the same. Sara stopped by the home one week, and she once again brought up the subject of adopting a dog. "Still not interested," he told her. But then she told him the story of Snoopy.

The little schnauzer had lived most of his life with one family. The kids had grown up and moved away, and Snoopy's human parents had fallen on some hard times during the recent economic recession. They decided to downsize and move closer to their children. Unfortunately, the condo complex they had chosen in their new city had a strict no-pets policy. They had to leave Snoopy behind.

The little dog was placed with a local shelter, but many families want to adopt a puppy, and Snoopy was already eight years old. Time and again, he was passed over in favor of a younger dog. Wouldn't Harry just come and take a look? He didn't need a dog, and he certainly didn't want a dog, but Snoopy's story pulled at Harry's heartstrings. He agreed to pay him a visit.

Sitting in the conference room at the shelter, Harry couldn't help but wonder what he was getting himself into. But when Snoopy was brought into the room, all he could think about was the little dog and what *he* was going through. Snoopy ran straight to Harry and promptly sat down. Tail wagging and head cocked, Snoopy seemed to be saying, "Where have you been?" How could Harry leave him there? And so he didn't.

It took a bit of an adjustment since Harry had never had a pet of his own, but by the week's end they were settled in. Snoopy was a model dog—sweet, trained, housebroken, and devoted. He was just happy to have a new home, and he showed his gratitude every day. He gave Harry wet little kisses and was trained to sit, come, roll over, and balance a treat on his nose. Best of all, Snoopy sat on Harry's lap and snuggled next to him in bed each night.

Studies show that owning a pet is beneficial for seniors. Pets can lower their owners' blood pressure and keep them active by taking walks. They provide companionship and unconditional love. And senior pets are even better for senior humans because of their calm and gentle disposition.

Harry may not have planned to get a pet, but he agreed to adopt Snoopy because it was in his nature to help someone in need. Before long, they were inseparable. Harry had a reason to get up each day, and little Snoopy had an owner to love. It was as if they had always been together. It may have taken eight years for them to connect, but these two were clearly made for each other.

Carry My Burdens

Lily got through the long and invasive surgery to remove both of her breasts. She was emotionally numb and had been feeling dazed ever since she was diagnosed with breast cancer and made the difficult decision to undergo a double mastectomy. Now, she had months of chemotherapy ahead of her. She knew cancer treatments would make her ill and fatigued and that she would not be able to work for a while, and she was worried about how she would get around.

It surprised Lily how many women she knew, including good friends and colleagues, who were being diagnosed with breast cancer. She had always prayed that this was one club she never would have to join. But here she was, facing a long and scary path ahead filled with uncertainties. For now, though, Lily just wanted to get through the first part of her recovery and mentally prepare for treatment.

During her first week at home, Lily could barely move from a sitting position and was in incredible pain despite the heavy medication she had been given. It helped, but she couldn't lift anything, prepare meals, or do much at all. She couldn't drive either, so she spent most of her time idly watching TV or reading. Lily was bored and longed to be active again, but she knew it would not be for quite some time.

Lily's mother and brother lived nearby and promised to be there as much as they could. Her mom, Alice, even offered to move in with Lily while she recovered, but Lily wanted to be alone. Besides, she had Marva, her loyal and loving Labrador retriever, to keep her company. Her mother would come over when Lily really needed her, but otherwise, Lily was determined to have as normal a life as she could, even while going through the nightmare of chemotherapy.

After chemo, Lily began to lose her hair and could barely move from the fatigue. She wanted to give up and give in to the cancer that she prayed was not still lingering in her body. But she did her best to muster up the courage, and somehow Lily made it through each day. Marva was there, guiding Lily into the kitchen or fetching her slippers. Marva was a big dog, and she was able to support Lily's body weight when Lily barely had the strength to shuffle back to bed. Sometimes Marva would grab the bedcovers and pull them over Lily when Lily could not do it herself, her muscles too sore and weak to move.

At night, Lily would often cry herself to sleep when her deepest fears seemed to come to the surface, and Marva was always there to snuggle up to her in bed and give her the companionship she needed during her loneliest, darkest moments. Marva  seemed to memorize Lily's schedule so that if Lily slept late, the dog barked or nudged her awake, reminding her of her next chemotherapy session. When her mom arrived to take Lily to her appointment, Marva always offered a bark of support as Lily left.

The months crept by slowly, and Lily was coming to accept the fact that hair loss and exhaustion were part of the price she had to pay to call herself a survivor. Her mother had talked her into joining a cancer support group for women at a nearby church, and Lily allowed her mom to drive her there one night a week to meet with other women who could relate and who knew exactly what she was enduring. Being around strong, happy, afraid, and honest women just like her helped Lily feel as if she could get through anything, even without the beautiful head of auburn hair she had come to think of as her best feature. She came to the realization that it was only hair and that nothing was more important than her health.

The support helped, and Lily felt stronger and more certain that she, like many of the survivors in the group, would beat cancer and begin the long road to recovery. She even scheduled the reconstructive surgery later that year. Through all of her decisions, Marva sat at her feet, letting Lily pet her and allowing Lily to feel the dog's strength and love. There were times when Lily would simply lean over, even though the pain was almost unbearable, and hug Marva, thanking her for being an affectionate and loyal friend. Not once did Marva ask for anything in return, and she never misbehaved. It was as if the dog knew how delicate the situation was, and Marva wanted nothing but comfort, peace, and ease for her beloved human. Marva stood beside her, ready to assist her, with nothing but unconditional love and concern in her big brown eyes.

Once the chemo treatment finally came to an end, Lily felt hopeful even though she knew that there was still so much ahead of her. Proudly showing her newly bald head in lieu of wearing a wig, Lily decided it was time to change a few things. She overhauled her diet and started to exercise more, taking Marva for walks and doing whatever she could to help her body not only heal but grow stronger and healthier. With the help of her family, friends, and especially Marva, Lily knew more than ever that she would not walk this path of recovery alone.

Two years later, Lily was officially cancer free when she received the devastating news that her beloved Marva had cancer. The dog was indeed old, and she would now need the same kind of love and support that she had given Lily. Together they got through Marva's surgery and treatments, but in the end the cancer took the dog's life. Lily was left heartbroken.

Lily's family planned a small memorial service for Marva, and Lily had the chance to speak about how her four-legged friend had been an essential part of her recovery and that Marva had showered Lily with the love and support she so desperately needed to become a cancer survivor.

As Lily grew stronger and the years passed with no return of breast cancer, she always made certain to thank God in her prayers for her friend and companion, Marva, who had been there to carry her burdens when she could not carry them herself.

Guardian Angel

When the Morrisons adopted King as a pet for their three children, they had no idea how big the shepherd-mix pooch would eventually get. Even as a puppy, King was large. And now, four years later, King was huge, with boundless energy that matched his size. But never once had King's hulking stature been an issue for the children. Their youngest, Jordan, had become King's best friend from the start. Jordan's siblings, 12-year-old Mara and 14-year-old Jamie, had little time for their pesky younger brother, but King always made 6-year-old Jordan feel like he was number one. The two were inseparable.

King took everything in stride, including letting the kids dress him up for Halloween or put reindeer antlers on him in the school Christmas play. King did everything with a happy outlook, his tail always wagging and a sparkle in his eyes. It was as if King were a kid himself. He was also the best watchdog, once protecting the family when a burglar attempted to break in the back patio door. The thief got a big surprise when the huge dog hurtled himself against the door, barking ferociously. The man took off like a rocket, and he was later caught by police. The Morrisons were forever grateful for King's courage and heroism.

When it was time for young Jordan to start first grade, he was terrified. He would be going to a new school and taking the bus with kids he didn't know. King waited on the corner with Jordan for the bus to arrive each morning and barked and jumped all over the boy when he returned home from school each afternoon. Just knowing King was there helped Jordan feel more confident and gave him something to look forward to. Soon, he was introducing King to his new friends at the bus stop, and he even brought King to school one day for show-and-tell.

Because Jordan was the youngest, King was very protective of the boy, going so far as to not let Jordan out of his sight when playing in the front yard. When Jordan would run up the street after his friends, King would follow along to keep an eye on him. When Jordan was hurt in a fall, King was the first on the scene, offering loving kisses and nudges until mom arrived with bandages and ointment. And when Jordan was sad or upset, King was right there at his side to console him with the big, dark eyes that promised eternal friendship.

Now and then, Jordan would become preoccupied with new friends coming over to play and forget about King. But King never took it too hard, and he often joined in on the playtime, to the boys' delight. And when he didn't join them, King watched his pal Jordan play from afar, ever at the ready to leap into action if Jordan was in danger or needed him. King loved and protected his entire family, but he and Jordan shared a very special bond, as if King knew that the youngest child needed the most protection of all.

Only once did King knock Jordan down, and it was by accident. The dog had been so excited to see Jordan when he returned from a sleepover at a friend's house that he knocked the little boy flat on his bottom when he came through the front door. Jordan had fallen hard on the tile and became angry and upset, even pushing King away at first. King was sad and howled until Jordan called for him after his mom reassured Jordan that it was just an accident. King ran to Jordan and licked him, rubbing his head against the boy's leg as if apologizing. When Jordan bent down to kiss King on the top of his head, all was forgiven and forgotten.

One day after school, King met Jordan at the bus stop as always, eager and ready to play with his best pal before Jordan had to do homework. Jordan got off the bus and heard a friend call his name from across the street. The boy ran into the street as the bus pulled away, and before anyone could stop him, King bolted after the boy. He lunged his entire body weight against Jordan and pushed him out of the street as a car sped by, missing Jordan completely. But King wasn't so lucky, and the car made contact, sending the dog hurtling through the air, landing on the hard pavement. Amidst the neighbors' screams and shouts, King fell limp to the ground and laid there. Jordan was still on the cold concrete as the neighbors shouted to Jordan's parents that the boy was okay, and they rushed out to see what had happened.

Jordan managed to get up, scraped and bruised but able to walk. When he went over to check on King, the dog was barely breathing. A few neighbors helped Mr. Morrison get King into the car, and the family sped off to the animal hospital a few blocks away. Jordan sat in the back with King's head resting on his lap, Jordan's tears falling onto the injured dog's face. King's eyes were closed, his breath shallow and gasping. By the time they reached the hospital, King was gone.

As the days went on, Jordan was totally in despair. He barely wanted to eat and rarely cracked a smile. The boy called out for King almost every night in his sleep, but there was no wagging tail and wet nose to respond. The Morrisons debated about getting another dog to help them all recover from the loss of their beloved King, but Jordan refused.

Mrs. Morrison thought it might help to have a ceremony to celebrate King's life and his love, devotion, and heroic act. She and a few neighbors planned a lovely and moving reception in the backyard of their house, and the entire neighborhood showed up, as well as some of the children's friends. At the ceremony, each family member said a few words about King, and there were pictures of the dog on display and a blank board that people signed with well wishes for King in heaven.

Jordan refused to participate at first, hiding in his room weeping. But from his bedroom window, he could hear the wonderful stories his family shared about King, and he eventually came down and sat in the backyard with everyone else. When the memorials were over, Jordan stood up and went to the front of the crowd. He could barely get out the words, but they came nonetheless. "King was my hero. I love you, King," said Jordan.

Every single person there wept fresh tears, but something shifted in Jordan as he came to accept that King was gone. He even mustered a few smiles when friends shared just how much they loved King's endless energy and antics.

A few months later, Jordan came to his parents and asked if they could adopt another dog. They were delighted to oblige, but Jordan insisted that their new friend not look anything like his old friend King. "There could be only one King," Jordan told them. And the entire family agreed.

From Abandoned to Adored

With patches of orange and brown fur and constantly squinting eyes, Nanny the kitten was barely old enough to eat on her own. Still, she was found abandoned on the street. As is the case with abandoned animals, the local shelter picked up little Nanny, which could have been the end of this kitten's life. However, one of the shelter workers knew of a kind person named Catherine who took on special cases like this little one.

It turned out that Nanny had been born with disfigured eyelids, and she was constantly squinting because of how irritated her eyes had become. This was likely the reason that the original owner abandoned her. Some people want only "perfect" pets.

Thanks to Catherine, who took Nanny into her home and welcomed her into the family, the kitty received drops in her eyes daily and corrective surgery on her eyelids when she was old

enough. Although they still do not look completely healed and "normal," her eyes no longer bother her to the point of constant whimpering and squinting.

Through all her discomfort and pain and the necessary treatment to relieve it, Nanny has never been anything but a truly happy kitten. It is as if she has no idea that there is anything wrong or different about her. She runs, jumps, and plays just like any other happy, healthy feline. Nanny loves being petted, snuggling, and curling up to Catherine for her daily snoozes. She climbs up Catherine's pant leg to oversee what's cooking on the stove, and the close supervision of her owner is exactly how she got her name. To say Nanny has personality is an understatement.

Because of all the things she has overcome, Nanny is now taken around to various local events by the family that adopted her. By her very presence, Nanny proves a point: Although a little different, she still has a big spirit and a loving personality to share. The colorful kitten has sat in the laps of small children as they learn to read, offering an encouraging purr or blink. She has been stroked and lovingly called "imperfectly perfect." Nanny has inspired people to see past her differences and realize that she and other special-needs animals like her are just as loving and deserving of a good home as any so-called "normal" pet.

People miss out when they demand perfection—in animals or in other people. Often there's far more joy to be found in someone who's a little different or has walked a more difficult road. That's what Nanny teaches us. This abandoned kitten turned into an adorable cat—and she is adored by not just her family, but by all who meet her and have a chance to pet those soft patches of orange and brown fur.

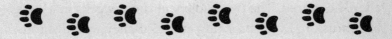

*Animals are such agreeable friends—they
ask no questions, they pass no criticisms.*

—George Eliot

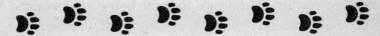

An Unlikely Truce

"Retirement does not have to be this boring," Carol told her nine-year-old Boston terrier, Bailey, a few weeks after she retired. The two had spent those weeks in a state of confusion. Every morning at 7:45, Bailey would stand by the back door to be let out for the day. When Carol would call her to come inside ten minutes later, Bailey would give her that "Who, me?" look. For the rest of the day, Bailey would pace around the house until 5:30 in the evening, the time Carol used to come home from work. Then Bailey would revert to her normal self, bringing toys for Carol to toss, snuggling with her on the sofa, and begging for treats.

"We need more action around here," Carol told Bailey. And according to Carol, what spelled action more than a kitten? She always wanted to adopt another furry friend, and she thought there was no better time than now.

Later that week, Carol set a half-grown feline fur ball she adopted from the shelter next to Bailey and said, "This is Dasher. Treat him gently."

Carol expected more out of Bailey than the dog's aggrieved-princess routine. Bailey would disdainfully sniff Dasher then yelp at the claw scratch the kitten gave her on the nose. When Dasher drank from Bailey's water bowl, Bailey would bark from a safe distance until he had lapped up his fill. The pooch refused to snuggle with Carol on the sofa when Dasher was on her lap.

Although the kitty was undaunted by living with a jealous dog, Carol bought Dasher a plush red cat bed so he could have a place of his own. As soon as it was unwrapped and set on the floor, Bailey occupied it. Her head hung off one end, her tail off the other. Dasher snatched one of Bailey's toys and played with it enthusiastically while Bailey glowered from the cat bed.

Carol finally had the "action" she was craving, but she felt badly that it was at her beloved dog's expense. One afternoon Carol pulled out the dog leash, which she thought would be the only thing that would get Bailey out of the cat bed, and the two headed out the door for the second love of Bailey's life: a walk. (Food had always been her first, but at this point Carol figured it might have been replaced by that cat bed.) Dasher slipped out the door and followed them. Carol couldn't catch Dasher to bring him back inside the house, and he refused to desert the group. Bailey plodded along the riverbank, tail drooping, too dispirited to bark at the geese Dasher was chasing.

Even though Carol's pets had not become the fast friends she had hoped they would be, eventually the two reached an uneasy truce. Each animal staked out and defended his or her own territory, and they seemed to be learning the basic rules of pet cohabitation. Carol's friends told her that it would be a kindness to her elderly dog to get rid of the cat, but by then Carol knew that Dasher had become a permanent part of their dysfunctional little family.

While Carol's atypical brood had certainly grown closer, it took a cooking disaster to make them a real family. One evening Carol was cooking chili for dinner when she forgot that it was heating on the stove, and the smell of smoke quickly alerted her that her meal was boiling over. The cornbread in the oven was also charred and smoke billowed from the oven when she opened it. The smoke detector shrieked.

While Carol was opening the windows and fanning the air with the cat bed, firemen alerted by a neighbor charged through the door. They hustled Carol out of the house so quickly that she did not have time to grab her purse. Bailey was trailing behind her, and the dog paced between Carol and the men in boots. Carol did not see flames licking curtains and walls, but the fire chief ordered her to stay outside. At that point Carol must have been too flustered to think about Dasher even when Bailey ran back inside. Bailey quickly returned with a snarling, clawing Dasher in her mouth. She dropped the cat at Carol's feet, sat beside her, and nudged her knee for a pat. Carol hugged and praised her heroic dog while Dasher stalked off to bother some birds that were congregating in the yard.

The cat bed still belongs to Bailey, but now the two furry pals play together and share the water bowl like collaborative colleagues, if not best friends. At night they snuggle with Carol on the sofa, one on each side. Carol's Christmas card photo surprised friends with whom she had shared stories about their domestic strife. In the photo, Carol is kneeling beside the Christmas tree with a dog on one side and a cat on the other, both wearing Christmas ribbon and rather pleasant expressions. The caption wrote itself: "All is calm."

Buck's Tender Side

"He's the one," Jane thought, staring into the eyes of the medium-size white dog at the local animal shelter. He looked like he was part white shepherd and part Lab. There was something sad about those eyes—something pleading—even more so than the other dogs they had seen that afternoon.

Days before Jane had said, "You've got to be kidding," when her husband, Steve, suggested that they get another dog. Having one dog was hard enough for her. Since she'd been bitten as a child, Jane had developed a fear and, at times, a hatred of dogs. She had seen them as mean, even wondering at times why God put them on the earth. "Certainly not for us to have as pets," she thought. Maybe they should just stay in the wild.

Their first dog, a Dalmatian, had confirmed Jane's "dogs are mean" theory by biting their five-year-old's ear. They gave him to Jane's sister, a dog lover with no children, and they now had Shadow, a beagle-shepherd mix. Jane felt proud of herself for adjusting to life with a dog in the house. But two dogs? She went to the animal shelter under protest.

Yet there, sitting across from her, was Buck. He wasn't barking like the other dogs. He was just looking intently at her, and she felt drawn to him. She and Steve took him outside with Shadow, whom they had brought along. The two dogs played a game of doggy tag, and Buck seemed to like their daughters, too, as he vigorously wagged his tail while they petted him.

Jane carefully studied the information card and discovered that the previous owners couldn't keep Buck anymore because he had dug his way out of their fenced yard. They would have to keep him on a leash. "We can break him of his digging habit," Jane told her husband optimistically.

Buck arrived at their house and seemed excited about his new surroundings. He chased their two younger cats but didn't seem to want to hurt them. He barked at Katy, their "queen" cat, who hissed at him from the safety of her perch on the back of the couch. But Buck's message seemed to be, "Can't we play and be friends?"

In the days ahead they found out that the trouble with Buck wasn't just digging, although he did enjoy that. They noticed that Buck had certain fears. If he was startled while sleeping, he would awaken in an attack mode. If anyone moved too quickly, he would lash out at them, opening his mouth and putting his teeth on them. He never drew blood, but it was disconcerting.

He also seemed obsessed with shoes—especially the athletic kind. Whenever someone would come into the house wearing white athletic shoes, Buck would charge at the shoes as if he were furious at them.

The family also discovered he was afraid of baseball caps. One day, Jane's nephew came into the house wearing one, and Buck lunged at him and tried to take the hat off with his mouth. At first glance, it looked as if he was going for her nephew's face.

Buck cowered when the girls played with a baseball bat in the yard. From Buck's behavior, they surmised that someone who wore athletic shoes and a baseball cap must have kicked Buck and possibly even hit him with a baseball bat or at least threatened him with one. This someone also might have kicked him when he was sleeping.

Jane and Steve considered giving Buck away, but who would take a dog that was so aggressive? They had known people who put a dog like Buck down because they thought he was dangerous. But he didn't seem dangerous to them—only scared. Yet, what if he snapped?

Jane discovered that when Buck wasn't scared, he was very loving. He cuddled up close whenever he got the chance, and he always seemed eager for tender words. When Jane would say, "Oh, Shadow, you're such a sweet doggy," Buck would come running from the other room and try to push Shadow out of the way and get close to her, with a "say-that-to-me" body wag. Even now, he loves to be petted and pushes his snout under any available hand to get some affection. When Jane lies in bed, he often jumps up and snuggles with her. Shadow is much more aloof, so she thinks it's great to have a dog who craves love and attention.

As Jane and Steve contemplated the possibility of giving up on Buck in his early days with them because of his negative behavior, Jane thought of the people she knew who had been abused in childhood. They too have behaviors rooted in fear. They overreact to situations because they're afraid of being hurt again. Jane had to admit that sometimes she wanted to give up on those relationships because they often snapped at her. Yet, as with Buck, they had never really hurt her—they had just startled her with their defensiveness.

As time went on, Jane learned things about Buck and about people who have been abused. Her first impulse when Buck switched to his fear mode was to scold him.

That didn't help at all; it only made him more afraid. She soon learned that talking tenderly to him calmed him down right away. Early on when she would take him out at night, fear would suddenly overtake him, and he would walk around cautiously as if something or someone was going to attack him at any moment. When he was in this mood, he refused to "do his duty." Jane would get so frustrated that she would shout, "Bucky, will you just go already?" Soon she learned that if she said in a loving way, "Oh, Bucky, you are such a good boy," he would snap out of his fear mode. Jane found that this works for people too. If they are afraid and acting strange because of it, lashing out at them doesn't help. Yet if she builds them up and says something kind, reminding them that she loves them, many times the fear goes away.

Buck loves other dogs and always seems eager to greet them on walks. Even if another dog is aggressive toward him, Buck rarely fights back. He just stands there or moves back a few steps. Jane and Steve do some dog-sitting, and Buck loves the "company." He also enjoys playing with Shadow, his "little sister." They run from room to room and then stop to wrestle on the carpet. Buck is never too rough with her, even though she's smaller. They seem to have an understanding. One or the other of them will snort during their wrestling matches and that means, "I've had enough" or "Let's rest a minute."

Buck's tenderness toward anyone who is hurting has also really struck Jane. One day at the vet, some boarding dogs were outside howling, and Buck let out sympathy howls in unison with them while Jane paid the bill. Then when they got outside, he went and licked each dog that was chained up. He's the same way when he knows that anyone in the house is upset. He wants to make sure he offers comfort—either with a concerned look, a lick, or a snuggle.

Jane and Steve have had Buck for more than five years now, and the longer they have him, the more they understand him. The more they show love to him, the less fearful he is and the more he trusts. Through Buck, Jane has learned to have compassion for and patience with people who have been hurt and who demonstrate fear. She has also realized God is that way toward everyone. Now Jane knows why God created dogs—and she knows why he gave Buck to them: To teach them some lessons in loving.

An Unstoppable Love

Sometimes the love between a pet and an owner is so strong that not even a potentially fatal injury can stop them from being reunited. That's what happened to a man named David Lechan and his faithful five-year-old German shepherd, Sage. Lechan and Sage were inseparable. Each day when he went to work, he knew that Sage would be there to happily greet him when he got home. That is, until one day when she wasn't there.

It all started on a chilly December day. Sage was out walking around and exploring their 40-acre wooded property in Dartmouth, Massachusetts, which she had done many times before. Sage must have heard a noise or seen something, and she ran off into the nearby woods to investigate. The German shepherd might have lost her way, because when Lechan returned home from work that evening, Sage was not there to greet him as she usually was. Dave immediately went looking for her, but he was unable to find any sign of her.

Lechan spent the next few days anxiously searching the property and the woods for his beautiful dog. When he still could not find his Sage, he began to give up all hope of ever seeing her again. Heartbroken, Lechan eventually ended the search, assuming his friend was gone for good.

On a Wednesday afternoon about a week later, Lechan returned home from work and took a walk to his barn to fetch something. He found Sage lying there waiting for him. As he greeted his dog, Dave was horrified to find that Sage had been shot. Although she must have been in severe pain, Sage forced herself to get up to greet her owner. Dave immediately went into action and drove her to the vet. Sage had eight entry wounds, one exit wound, and plenty of shrapnel lodged in her body, some of which they could not get out. The veterinarian determined that Sage had been left for dead in the woods, alone and bleeding for an entire week, surviving on swamp water and the sheer determination to get back home. Sage had not lost too much weight, thankfully, and she was somehow able to withstand the elements long enough to find her way home.

And find her way back home she did, dragging her weak and injured body through the woods and all the way across Lechan's property to the barn, where she waited for Lechan to find her. Through the pain, fear, and physical struggle, Sage continued on with only one goal in mind: to get back to where she belonged. Luckily, Sage made a full recovery and will perhaps think twice about running off into the woods on her own the next time curiosity gets the best of her.

A dog is the only thing on earth that loves you more than he loves himself.

—Josh Billings

A Pigheaded Rescue

Not everyone is a pig lover. In fact, many people think of pigs as mud-loving animals who are better left on the farm. But don't ever say that to William, because according to him, "man's best friend" would certainly be a pig.

To be fair, a pig is not a pet that William would have chosen for himself. His grandchildren felt differently, however, and that's where it all began. The kids learned about pot-bellied pigs in school and thought that one would make a fantastic house pet. The family had a big house with a lot of land and plenty of room for a pig to run. After months of begging and pleading, the two youngsters convinced their mom and dad to let them get a pig. They named her Penny.

The entire family fell in love with Penny. As it turns out, pigs—and Penny in particular—are very intelligent animals. She quickly acclimated to home life, learning commands and tricks just as a canine would. Penny did what she was asked, walked on a leash, and was curious and very affectionate.

William eventually met Penny, and he soon conceded that pigs weren't so bad after all.

That same year, William's son was offered a job in New York City. That meant the family was going to live in an apartment in a high-rise building. There would be plenty of space for a family of four, but unfortunately it wasn't the place to raise a pig.

As expected, William was called upon to adopt the family pet. And according to William, it was the best thing that ever happened to him. Penny and William quickly became the best of buddies. Penny followed him everywhere and often slept at the side of his bed. William was entertained by how strangers reacted when they saw Penny, and the pair became a familiar sight walking up and down the streets of the small town. People would call out to the two in passing, and William was always more than happy to stop for conversation and a few pets or a treat for the jovial little piglet.

It was a hot summer night when Penny was really put to the test. She had gone to sleep on the porch because the heat inside was too much for a pig to handle. In the morning when she went inside to wake William, she couldn't get his attention. He seemed to be asleep, but his breathing was irregular. Penny ran from room to room and seemed to sense that something was wrong—not just with William but also with the house itself. She tried again to rouse her owner by pushing him with her snout and licking his hand. Finally his eyes fluttered open, but he was unable to get up.

Penny took matters into her own hands (or hooves) and scurried outside. There were no neighboring homes within view, so the pot-bellied pig did the next best thing: She lay down in the street to attract passing cars. The first car swerved to miss the pig, but it kept going. The next driver stopped, concerned that the pig was sick or injured. When the driver got out of the car, Penny sprang up and ran toward the house. The surprised driver walked cautiously toward the house while Penny ran back and forth, indicating for him to follow. When the man reached the house and went inside, he smelled the gas right away. As soon as he saw William, he dragged him outside and called 9–1–1. Penny's shrewdness saved her owner's life.

Hearing a story of a heroic cat or dog isn't exactly rare, but William wouldn't trade his pot-bellied pig for all the money in the world. According to her proud owner, this is one Penny that's worth her weight in gold.

Mountain Climbing in the Multipurpose Room

Emma watched Bobby, a small boy with bright red hair and freckles, face the wall and slowly make his way around the perimeter of the school's multipurpose room. His walk was uneven and jerky as he carefully examined objects in the air—objects visible only to him. Bobby took great pains to avoid eye contact with anyone, but he often stole quick glances over his shoulder to see what was going on.

Friendly therapy dogs were being petted, brushed, and walked by Bobby's fellow students. The dogs and their trained handlers, Emma included, had come to the James J. McBride Special Education Center in Los Angeles for their monthly visit. Everyone was having a great time. Everyone but Bobby.

The school was filled with children who had a wide range of disabilities, from autism, like Bobby, to cerebral palsy or Down syndrome. But even at McBride, where being different was the norm, Bobby was an outsider.

Emma watched as the nine-year-old made his way around the large room, separating himself from his peers, the therapy dogs, his teachers, and the volunteers. Was it by choice or habit? Did he want to join in? What was he thinking when he saw Mariella in her hot pink wheelchair, a wide smile on her face, walking Bosco, a spunky beagle? Did he want to walk a dog, too? What thoughts crossed his mind as he watched six-year-old Marta and seven-year-old Thomas brush a docile black Lab named Virgil, who never flinched when the brushes missed their mark and raked his floppy ears or wet nose? Bobby glanced at Garbo, a snazzy silver schnauzer wearing a leather jacket, and he noticed his classmates getting pictures taken with their therapy-dog pals. Did Bobby want his picture taken, too?

Bobby's quick glances became lingering looks. As Emma watched this child from the corner of her eye, she thought she saw something—a longing to join in but with no way to get there. Emma went over to him with Bosco the beagle and held out the leash. "Hi, Bobby, would you like to walk this dog? His name is Bosco." Bobby flinched in stiff defiance, turned away, and said, "No!" Emma left him alone. So did everyone else. Maybe just being in the room was the best he could do.

During her next several visits, Emma tried to involve Bobby again. He would come to the room and cautiously observe the therapy dogs in action. But he was far more comfortable staying near the walls than sitting on the floor and petting a dog.

On their last visit for the school year, the multipurpose room was brimming with happy children and the therapy dogs with whom they'd become friendly and familiar. Fears had been overcome: Robbie, once hesitant to talk, told Virgil a secret. Grace, who had been afraid to touch any dog, now gave each pooch a big hug. And Mariella was helped out of her wheelchair and into a walker so she could walk her favorite dog, a sandy-colored pug named Dogtor Buddha.

After the therapy dogs and volunteers spread out on the floor and the children came into the room, Emma spotted Bobby doing his perpetual dance around the perimeter of the room. The walls were his friends.

Emma's 14-year-old nephew, Nick, an experienced volunteer trained in animal-assisted therapy, had come to school that day with Molly, a golden retriever therapy dog. As Nick helped Thomas brush Molly's silky fur, a boy came up to Emma and sat down close beside her. It was Bobby. She welcomed him and touched his shoulder, and he didn't flinch. He picked up a book she had and asked her to read it to him. The short picture book was about puppies. As Emma read, Bobby listened and studied the illustrations, turning the pages at exactly the right moment. Then he asked her to read it again. And again.

Ten times was enough. Emma asked Bobby if he wanted to walk Molly. He thought about it, looked away, and answered, "Cheese."

Nick knew what Bobby wanted. "Okay, Bobby, come here, and I'll take your picture with Molly." Bobby got up and stood near Molly, not too close, but close enough to be in the frame. Bobby held the Polaroid photo on the white edge and, as he watched it develop, a smile spread across his face.

"You can take that picture home," Emma told him. It was tangible proof that progress shows up when one least expects it. Sometimes it just takes a little longer to develop.

Bobby carefully put the photo of Molly and himself in the front pocket of his shirt. He patted it to make sure it was safe. He looked around the room at the other dogs, the children, his teacher, and the volunteers. He was miles from any wall.

Matchmaker

It had been four years since Ron's wife, Annie, had passed away from ovarian cancer. He missed her, and had it not been for the companionship of his fawn-colored pug, Rufus, he wasn't sure how he would have dealt with the loneliness. Rufus mourned Annie's loss as well, but since then the quirky pug was always at Ron's side, ready to offer a simple wag of a tail when he knew his owner was feeling down.

Ron loved the walks he and Rufus took each day, and he cherished the way Rufus always seemed to know just when he most needed companionship, especially at night. The nights were still difficult. When Ron missed Annie, he would call for Rufus, and the two would play fetch before turning in for the night. Rufus would snore at the foot of the bed, a pleasant reminder to Ron that despite grief, life goes on.

But Ron missed the companionship of a woman to love even though he balked at the idea of getting back into the dating pool. Ron felt uncertain how to even go about navigating the world of online dating sites, and he refused to go to singles bars. He met a few women through his job in broadcasting, but he could never muster up the courage to begin dating again until a lovely woman named Sandy moved in next door.

Sandy was about Ron's age, single, and she always smiled and called out a friendly hello to Ron and Rufus as they passed her house on their daily walks. Often they would stop for a minute to chat, and Rufus would sit at Ron's feet, looking happily from Ron to Sandy with his tail wagging back and forth. Sandy almost always had a treat in hand for Rufus since she had her own dog, a poodle named Sadie who usually came outside to greet them as well.

Ron thought Sandy was lovely, and he was touched when she left freshly baked cookies on his doorstep one day while he was at work. He had meant to go thank her, but he hadn't yet had a chance. So one day Rufus decided to take matters into his own hands. He snuck through a gap in the backyard fence while Ron was away, and the pug went to pay Sandy and Sadie a visit.

When Ron returned home that evening, he found a note on his door telling him to stop by Sandy's. Sandy answered the door looking pretty as always with a big smile on her face. "Someone stopped by my house today," she said, and Rufus came bounding into view with Sadie on his tail. Rufus barked and jumped all over Ron, panting and wagging his tail as if to tell him something. Ron blushed and apologized for his behavior, but Sandy simply laughed. There was an awkward moment of silence before Ron took Rufus and both said their good-byes.

Two days later, Ron came home to another note from Sandy, and he couldn't help but laugh. When Sandy greeted him at the door, the most delicious smells wafted toward Ron. Ron could see that she was cooking dinner, and he apologized for bothering her to fetch his mischievous pup. He was about to go scold Rufus when the dog bounded in the room and jumped up to lick his face before running off with Sadie to play.

Ron opened his mouth to apologize yet again, but Sandy just smiled and invited him in. He kept calling to Rufus, who refused to come, and Ron was a bit flustered about the dog's bad behavior. "He's never done this before," he told Sandy, and that's when she leaned in and whispered, "I think he has a thing for Sadie." She winked at Ron, who blushed again and smiled back. Ron promised to have Rufus out of her hair before her dinner date arrived, but Sandy turned around to stir something on the stove and said in a playful tone, "Oh, my dinner date is already here." She turned and flashed him another smile, and that's when Ron realized that he had been set up by a fawn-colored matchmaker with four paws.

Dinner was delicious, and the beginning of a beautiful friendship between Ron and Sandy soon evolved into something even more wonderful. Ron learned that Sandy lost her husband just two years prior, and that she, too, had dreaded the thought of returning to the world of bad dates and wasted time. The pair had much in common, and they shared the same values as well as a love for the dogs that had helped each of them get through some dark and lonely times. Their relationship blossomed, and all because of a dog who played matchmaker better than any of Ron's friends ever could have. As for Rufus, he continues to sneak over to visit his furry friend, Sadie, although for the most part, he is always invited.

Who Says Cats Don't Care?

Zipper was one of two dogs that lived on the Jensen farm along with his canine sister, Molly. The two were born in the same litter and were indisputably the best of friends. When Molly got sick, it was a cat that took matters into her own paws to make Zipper's life worth living again.

From the earliest weeks, when they would tumble over each other to get to their mother's milk, Zipper and Molly were inseparable. The family who owned the farm sold four of the puppies from their litter, but they knew better than to try to separate these two.

For 12 years Zipper and Molly were a dynamic duo. They ate together, they snuggled together, and they played together. Where one went, the other followed. They got along with the cats living on the farm, but neither paid them much attention. Why should they? They had each other.

One day Molly became sick. She lived another three weeks, and at the ripe old age of 84 in dog years, she passed away. Of course the Jensens were sad to lose their beloved pooch, but Zipper was devastated. Without his best friend, he moped around the farm as if life were barely worth living. He rarely ate, and he certainly didn't want to play. The only thing he did was sleep all day long.

The Jensens were worried about Zipper. He was, after all, the same age as Molly, and he seemed to have lost his cheerful and buoyant personality. He was losing weight, and his once-mischievous eyes were now clouded over. The Jensens weren't sure what to do.

Around that time, Cassie, a black-and-white Persian cat, started to pay attention to Zipper. She would bring him valuable gifts— like mice that she carried in her mouth—and gently lay them at his feet. She would take her nap by him and follow him whenever he ventured outside. She would even carry bits of cat food to his bowl, and Cassie would eat during those rare times that Zipper ate.

At first Zipper ignored the cat, but little by little he began to take an interest in her—and in his life again. The first step was eating some of his food, which gave him strength. In time, he slowly started to play again, either with his new feline friend or the other animals in the Jensen menagerie.

Zipper, the dog that had shared so much with his littermate, suddenly had a new best friend. Whether he realized that his new friend was feline rather than canine is unknown. Whatever the reason, the now 13-year-old Zipper is living the life of a much younger dog. All because of a cat that cared.

Let Hercules himself do what he may,
The cat will mew and dog will have his day.

—*William Shakespeare*

Bunny Hops to Owner's Rescue

No one was allowed to have animals in the senior apartment complex. But Grace had owned Bunny since the rabbit was born, and she wasn't about to abandon her when she moved in. And it's a good thing she didn't, because Bunny brought her more than just luck—Bunny saved her life.

Ten years earlier, a friend's rabbit was about to have a litter of kits. Grace remembered having rabbits when she lived in the country as a little girl, and she thought a bunny might make a good pet. She didn't have the time for a dog, and cats had a reputation of being aloof. A rabbit seemed like a suitable compromise; they were easier to take care of and more affectionate.

So Grace jumped in with both feet, ready to become a mom to a little bunny. The situation worked out just the way she had hoped. She bought a cage, food, and toys and was ready to train

Bunny to use the litter box. Bunny was smart, and Grace was able to train her easily. The rabbit was the perfect companion.

After Grace retired, she decided that living in a senior community would suit her. She would meet other people her age and say goodbye to mowing her lawn, raking the leaves, and shoveling snow. She had already signed on the dotted line when she discovered that she wasn't supposed to have a pet. A rabbit, she decided was a *small* pet. She was quiet, she didn't destroy things, and Grace wouldn't have to walk past the other apartments to take her outside. Who would even know?

Grace and Bunny moved into their new home, a quaint and cozy place for the two of them. Bunny adjusted quickly, and the duo went about their daily routine as usual: eat, play, snuggle, and enjoy each other's company. Because she had adjusted so well to the litter box, Grace let Bunny run loose while they were home alone. And that was what saved Grace's life.

Grace had gone downstairs to fetch her mail when she started to feel a pain in her chest. It quickly moved to her left shoulder, and Grace found herself unable to catch her breath. She had just stepped into her apartment when she fell to the ground, feeling a crushing pain in her chest. She was having a heart attack.

Bunny crept to her side and sensed that Grace was in danger and needed help. Fortunately, the door was still ajar, and Bunny hopped out to the hallway where she was confronted by several closed doors. She began to hop up and down the hallway, making as much noise as she could. Grace would later recall that the little rabbit managed to sound like a herd of elephants charging through the hallway.

Apparently her next-door neighbor, Mary, agreed, because she opened her door to find what the commotion was all about. At first she didn't see anyone, but then she felt something pounce on her foot. Mary looked down, and there sat the frantic Bunny. If seeing a rabbit in the apartment hallway was a surprise, then finding one who clearly had something on her mind was a complete shock. Bunny moved quickly back to Grace's door, and Mary followed. Mary was able to call 9–1–1, and Grace was transported to the hospital before any real damage occurred.

The bad news? Grace's secret pet was no longer a secret. But the good news far outweighed the bad. If not for Bunny, Grace might have died that day. The best news? Grace was allowed to keep her lifesaving pet. Bunny became something of a mascot to the seniors who delighted in spoiling the little heroine with carrots. This was one secret Grace was glad to have out of the bag.

Mae, the Hospice Volunteer

At 86 years old, Anna's childless Aunt Esther entered the last phase of her life with dignity and acceptance. She asked Anna, her closest relative, to accompany her on what she called her last journey, and she promised Anna—and perhaps herself—that she would go gently.

Standing in her living room, 600 miles away from Esther's house, Anna looked down at her puppy, Mae. Mae was a frisky nine-month-old black Labrador, and she was finishing off Anna's most precious pair of Italian shoes she had purchased on vacation in Florence the summer before. Mae had already turned Anna's Italian handbag into rawhide and eaten a section of floorboard. According to Mae, toilet paper was to be unrolled and festooned around the house, food on the table had her name on it, and guests were moving targets to be jumped on. Other than that, Anna thought she was a good companion.

When Anna was ready to leave to accompany her sick aunt for the unknown number of weeks she would need her, she knew she had nowhere to leave Mae while she was away. The only option was to bring the puppy along. Mae hopped into the passenger seat with a large rawhide bone in her mouth, and Anna just hoped it would keep her from snacking on the dashboard of the car.

When Anna arrived at Esther's house, she put Mae in the backyard before going to the nursing home where her aunt had been staying since she was discharged from the hospital. Anna prayed that with the help of hospice, her presence would make Esther's final weeks more pleasant.

It was a warm and sunny day, and Mae had no complaints about her new play area. As soon as Anna let Mae loose in the yard, Mae ran the perimeter of the picket fence and barked as if to claim the territory. But Anna drove away only to see Mae in her rearview mirror, trailing behind her after she somehow managed to slip through the fence. Anna turned back to the house and let Mae climb in the backseat to accompany her to the nursing home.

Aunt Esther looked frail, but her blue eyes were bright. Anna was relieved that her mind was still sharp. The hospice nurse met with them, and they agreed that having Mae at the house, though a hyper and high-spirited puppy, was not necessarily a bad idea. But Anna was still worried. At this stage of her illness, Esther's weight had dropped below 80 pounds. Anna knew that even with the use of a walker, Esther was not safe from Mae's exuberant greetings. The nurse gave Anna the name of a local pet hotel just in case.

Anna left Mae in the car with the windows cracked open for the rest of the day while she got her Aunt Esther back to the house and situated in the living room. She sat her aunt down in the comfortable recliner chair located in a sunny corner of the room and put a glass of lemonade on the table beside her and a small plate of her favorite sugar cookies she had brought from home. Finally, Anna got Mae from the car and led her into the house. With Mae on a very short leash, Anna introduced them.

Mae had not yet learned to sit on command, so Anna didn't expect today to be any different. Instead the puppy padded slowly to her aunt's side and positioned herself for a pat on the head. "This is the little terror you've been talking about, Anna?" Esther asked in her gentle voice. "She seems more like an angel to me." Anna nodded, amazed that Mae sat still while her aunt slowly scratched behind her ears.

"She ate the shoes I bought in Florence," Anna said, "I'll have to watch her every second."

Esther was quiet and looked lost in thought. Anna realized that their pace of conversation and activity would be slow. Finally, Esther turned to Anna and said, "Take Mae to my closet and let her pick out a pair of shoes. No slippers." Anna knew that there was no need to discuss the obvious fact that Esther would not need the shoes again.

Esther's closet was neatly arranged by season. Mae looked at the plethora of shoes and then at Anna. "Go for it," said Anna. Mae looked hesitant, but she soon settled into the job. She sniffed each shoe then crammed a pair of black suede dress pumps in her mouth. They looked expensive. "Good taste, girl," Anna whispered.

Anna followed Mae back to the living room and was amazed to see her drop the shoes beside Esther and resume her position beside her chair. Esther patted her head. "Were you perhaps exaggerating her behavior to make me laugh?" she asked Anna.

Anna shook her head and willed the tears not to fall down her cheeks. Somehow Mae's hopeful gift of shoes had unlocked some of the sadness that, before then, Anna had been able to keep to herself. But she did not want to distress her aunt with her sorrow, and she did not let herself cry.

"Thank you for bringing Mae," Esther said. "She will make our time together even nicer."

And somehow Mae did. She ran around the backyard like a doggy Olympics contender, but in the house she was gracious and demur. She greeted each visitor, accompanied them to the living room, and quietly sat beside Anna's aunt.

Esther was bedridden by the next week, and Mae sat beside her, resting her chin on the colorful quilt that had been in the family for generations. Mae didn't knock anything over nor did she slobber on the heirloom quilt. She moved slowly as if sensing the seriousness of the situation. The hospice nurse was impressed, and she gave Mae a red bandanna with a white cross stitched on it. Anna took the bandanna off when Mae went outside to play, hoping that Mae would associate her bandanna with her newfound gentleness and decorum.

Aunt Esther died peacefully one dawn two weeks later with Anna and her "angel" Mae by her side. She went gently and without pain, as she'd promised, but Anna felt hollow inside.

After the funeral and settling her aunt's estate, the hollowness rode home with Anna and Mae. Mae was glad to be home, and she quickly decorated the house with toilet paper while Anna unpacked. When Mae started nibbling on Anna's favorite winter boots, she snatched them from the puppy's chops and made a decision: dog obedience school.

Mae was an excellent student, and Anna learned quickly that she herself needed training as well. Toward the end of the eight-week session, Anna told the trainer about the gentleness and devotion Mae had showed toward her aunt. The trainer suggested that Anna contact the local hospice association to see if Mae could be of use to them somehow.

And she was. Mae made many patient visits wearing her red bandanna. She left home as if she had a sense of purpose, and she always returned dipping her head so Anna could remove the bandanna. The local hospice nurse laughed about the ruined Italian shoes and informed Anna that she had told that story to her patients. "Mae did that?" they would ask. "Sweet, angelic Mae?"

"She's a reformed Labrador," Anna told her with a chuckle.

Mess-Kitt, the VIP Cat

Elaine was a U.S. Army nurse during World War II, serving with the 131st General Hospital at Blandford Camp close to Bournemouth, England. She was honored to serve her country and especially proud of the soldiers, who gave their all for the cause.

During Elaine's tour of duty, a mother cat chose to have her litter near the camp's kitchen. Elaine asked for permission to keep one of the kittens and chose a long-haired, striped one, which she named Mess-Kitt. She was a lively kitty who often got Elaine in trouble by scattering the contents of her wastebasket throughout the barracks. But she was worth the trouble. Mess-Kitt learned to meet her when she got off duty, which always brightened Elaine's day. She would get down on one knee, and Mess-Kitt would jump from that knee to her shoulder and curl around her neck like a fur piece. It was a blessing to have something to write home about other than the war.

Mess-Kitt enjoyed the care packages Elaine received, especially the canned Vienna sausages. Elaine used the cartons as litter boxes, filling them with sandy ground from a nearby field.

Sometimes Mess-Kitt would visit Elaine's ward. There she'd spend the day with "her boys," the wounded soldiers. They were alone, injured, and in a foreign country. They desperately needed someone to love, and Mess-Kitt filled that void, giving them something to think about besides the war.

One day Mess-Kitt started to have a seizure, and Elaine asked the colonel for permission to call a vet, even though she knew this would be a luxury that probably wouldn't be allowed. Imagine Elaine's surprise when he sent his own driver to take the ailing Mess-Kitt for treatment. It was clear that this morale-boosting kitty had worked her way into even the colonel's heart.

When the war eventually ended, it was time for Elaine to go home. She sadly gave Mess-Kitt to a friend she had met while in England, who wrote to Elaine for years after that, keeping her up-to-date on Mess-Kitt's mischievous antics.

So if anyone should hear some elderly veteran telling stories about a cat that comforted him in an Army hospital in England during the war, they should believe him—he's telling the truth.

Elaine is still proud of all of her boys who served, and she's just as proud of Mess-Kitt, one of God's small creatures who never stopped bringing love and joy to those who needed it most.

Thousands of years ago, cats were worshiped as gods. Cats have never forgotten this.

—Anonymous

Maddie and Mowie

Children are generally thought to be more sensitive to spirits and ghosts (if there are such things) than adults. Maybe it's because they are more open and accepting; they're too innocent to be jaded or skeptical of things around them.

If ghosts do exist, it would make sense that the ones that surround us are the spirits of people who care about our welfare. They could be people we knew in real life or ancestors looking out for us. One little girl can attest that there's another type of ghost that means us no harm—the spirit of a beloved pet.

Maddie was only two years old when her family brought home a fluffy little puppy they named Mowie. The miniature American Eskimo pup was a round ball of fur and the perfect size to scamper around the house after a busy toddler. It was only natural that they became the best of buddies.

When Maddie was old enough for a "big girl bed," Mowie would sleep on the floor beside it to keep her safe.

This lasted about two hours before Maddie decided that she would feel safer if the little dog was in the bed with her. Predictably, there was no going back after that. It was Maddie and Mowie's bed from that moment on.

The duo were inseparable. When Maddie had a tea party, Mowie got a cookie. When Mowie needed a walk, Maddie held the leash. When it was time for Mowie's bath, Maddie worked hard to get her clean, both of them playing with the soap bubbles that floated around the bathroom. And each night at bedtime, Maddie would get into her pajamas and Mowie would hop up and settle into her place at the end of the little girl's bed.

When Maddie grew a little older, she developed asthma. Ever devoted, Mowie added the job of protector to her current roles of playmate and friend. When Maddie had trouble breathing, Mowie would bark to alert the little girl's parents to come running. Fortunately, the condition was brought under control, and with Mowie's help, Maddie lived day to day quite comfortably.

Then one day, Maddie noticed that Mowie was not acting like her usual self. She was moping around the house, and the always-famished dog was now uninterested in her food. The family kept an eye on her for a few days before taking her to the vet. The news was not good: Mowie had cancer.

It was Maddie's turn to be the protector. The two had spent ten years together, and Maddie wasn't going to abandon Mowie now. The little girl spent every minute trying to make her canine friend a little more comfortable. She put Mowie's pills in peanut butter because she knew it was one of Mowie's favorite treats. She sat down on the floor while Mowie ate a little bit of food, and when she stopped, Maddie would encourage her to eat a little bit more.

Within a few short months, Mowie peacefully passed away in her sleep. The house was quiet and empty without the little dog clicking through the halls, and Maddie was devastated without her best friend.

Soon Maddie started to notice peculiar signs that her canine friend was not all that far away. A shadow in the hallway. A dog toy moved out of the basket. A dog-shape imprint on her bed, right where Mowie used to lie. When Maddie mentioned these sightings to her parents, they didn't believe her. It wasn't that they didn't want to believe her, but they were adults after all, and adults don't usually believe in ghosts. They thought the little girl was imagining Mowie because she wanted so badly to believe that the dog was still there.

One night, about two months after Mowie passed away, Maddie went to bed as usual. It was taking her a little longer to fall asleep these days without her canine companion by her side, but she finally did. Around midnight, Maddie woke up and started to cough. She felt like she couldn't breathe, and the more she tried, the harder it was to catch her breath.

Within seconds her parents were roused from a deep sleep by the sound of a dog barking. As the barks became louder and more insistent, Maddie's parents jumped from their bed and ran to Maddie's bedroom. They found her in the midst of an asthma attack and called 9–1–1. Paramedics arrived and eased Maddie's breathing before taking her to the hospital where she spent the night. She was going to be fine.

Maybe ghosts do exist. Maybe they don't. But one thing is certain: Both of Maddie's parents heard a frantic barking that sounded just like Mowie. It seems the little dog stayed around long enough to protect her best friend one more time. Her job was done, and now she could move on.

That Christmas Maddie came downstairs to find a small bundle of fur peeking out from under a giant red ribbon. It was a new puppy, and they named her Mowie.

Ginger and the Grouch

Every neighborhood has one: a grouch whose yard is only entered by children acting on a dare. Kim, Peter, and their two children lived next to him, and his name was Joe Lutz. Mr. Lutz's wife died a long time ago, and every day he would sit in a creaky old rocking chair on his front porch and glare at passing cars, children, and every living thing that came near. Before her children became toddlers, Kim had given up on offering cheery greetings that Mr. Lutz never returned and plates of homemade chocolate-chip cookies that were left on his porch until raccoons devoured them.

When the children were old enough to play outside on their own, Kim and Peter had been advised by their neighbors not to let the children set foot on Mr. Lutz's property. Kim never thought that he would hurt them, but she didn't want the children to contribute to his always-apparent misery.

As the children grew older and more active in their pre-teen years, Kim's husband pointed out that the next logical step for the family would be to adopt a dog.

Ginger was a 2-year-old mixed breed with long, puffy hair, floppy ears, and a tail that wagged at the least provocation. Ginger quickly associated the word "cookie" with a dog treat and expected one when she completed her morning chore of walking the kids to the bus stop. Kim would have her morning cup of coffee, and Ginger would eat her treat in doggy bliss. Ginger would then go outside and play in the grassy open space on the empty lot in their cul-de-sac that she usually wandered off to.

One morning, Kim noticed Ginger was late returning from the bus stop. She grabbed a sweater and headed out the door. Maybe the bus was late, or worse, maybe there was an accident at the formerly vacant lot that had recently been turned into a construction site.

When she was halfway down the steps, Kim spotted Ginger. She was sitting beside Mr. Lutz, who was rocking in his creaky chair with the usual sullen expression on his face. He didn't see Kim, and she tiptoed back inside the house utterly bewildered. Kim didn't think Mr. Lutz would harm Ginger, but she couldn't imagine the man ever wanting or allowing a dog on his porch.

Ginger came home about an hour later, and Kim wished the dog could talk so she could tell her about her visit.

The next day, Ginger once again did not return from the bus stop. And once again Kim spotted the pooch on Mr. Lutz's porch, where the old man was petting her soft ginger-hued fur.

Autumn progressed that year without much change except for the dying leaves. Ginger would walk the kids to the bus stop and then visit Mr. Lutz. Meanwhile, an unsightly orange fence went up around the construction site in the cul-de-sac.

One afternoon Kim looked outside and found Mr. Lutz standing on the sidewalk near the construction site, and he was shouting emphatically at a few members of the construction crew. Ginger followed Kim outside and rushed to Mr. Lutz's side. The argument grew louder and more heated. She was afraid Mr. Lutz would have a heart attack, and Ginger was baring her teeth. It looked as if Ginger had discovered her inner guard dog.

"What's going on here?" Kim asked a muscular construction worker.

"Seems he called the police," the man said. "Something about dog abuse? I think the police ignored him, because he says he called them yesterday, too."

Ginger stood between Mr. Lutz and the construction crew. For the first time, Kim heard her snarl.

"Mr. Lutz," Kim said. "What's the problem?"

"Problem!" he yelled. "It's an outrage! Building this cheap stack of bricks and a fence?" Mr. Lutz patted Ginger on the top of her head. "Now Ginger won't have any place to play!"

Ginger whined toward the construction crew, and Kim was speechless. Kim managed to get Ginger and Mr. Lutz away from the construction site and back to his porch. Mr. Lutz sat down, his rocker creaking against the old wood floor, and Ginger settled down next to him.

Even though Kim wondered why she should waste her time softening up to the old man, she couldn't deny the fact that Mr. Lutz and Ginger had formed a peculiar bond. "Would you like to walk Ginger once in a while?" she asked. "That way she won't miss her playground so much."

Mr. Lutz scratched his head. "Now there's a thought," he replied. "I could walk the children to the bus stop with Ginger, then walk around the block a time or two."

Ginger wagged her tail in response, and she kept Mr. Lutz company until lunchtime.

When Peter returned home from work that evening, Kim told him about their eventful day. Her husband was just as surprised as she was about Mr. Lutz's gentle behavior toward their dog, and the children reluctantly agreed to include Mr. Lutz in their daily routine.

Every school day after that, Mr. Lutz waited on the sidewalk for Ginger and the children with a dog treat in his hand, his angry expression replaced by a pleasant grin.

And if Kim ever had doubts about how much a dog could change an elderly man's spirit, she would remind herself of the morning when she heard her son say, "Come on, Ginger! Uncle Joe is waiting!"

Staunch and faithful little lovers that [dogs] are, they give back a hundred fold every sign of love ever given them.

—*Edith Wharton*

Saved by a Belle

Belle is one of a small number of dogs that get the opportunity to fly to Washington, D.C., meet with their congressperson, and accept a number of medals and awards for being loyal and helpful canines. Belle is not an ordinary dog. Ask Kevin Weaver, who owes his life to the beagle and her fast thinking and quick action.

At 34 years old, Kevin went into a diabetic seizure at his home in Ocoee, Florida, and collapsed onto the floor, unable to move or help himself. He fell unconscious, and his dog Belle came to the rescue, grabbing Kevin's cell phone and biting down on the number 9, which Kevin had programmed to dial 9–1–1 in case of an emergency. When an operator answered, Belle began to bark into the phone. When the dispatcher sensed that something horrible might be happening to someone on the other end of the line, help was immediately dispatched.

Kevin woke up hours later in a hospital bed, disoriented and weak. There was Belle, sitting at his bedside. He was later told that the pooch even managed to hitch a ride in the ambulance.

Kevin's doctor told him that Belle and her quick action had saved his life, and that without Belle's help he would have been left alone for far too long with dangerously low blood-sugar levels. Thankfully, he was not alone. Belle was there to help.

As a puppy, Belle had been returned twice to the same pet store by different buyers, both mysteriously unhappy with her before Kevin came along. Kevin was a flight attendant, and he adopted Belle at the suggestion of a friend. He took her home because he said he felt sorry for the twice-returned puppy, and the two became fast friends.

As Kevin's diabetes worsened, he became increasingly concerned for his health. He took the advice of one of his regular passengers, who suggested he have Belle trained as a medical-assistance dog. Little did he know how the training would one day pay off and save his life.

Because of Belle's heroism, the little beagle became the first animal to receive the VITA Wireless Samaritan Award, presented by the Cellular Telephone International Association Wireless Foundation to honor those who use mobile phones to save lives, help in emergency situations, or stop and report crimes in progress. Thanks to Kevin's devoted dog, her training, and his cell phone, he was indeed saved by a Belle.

More Than a Pretty Face

Amy had to agree that the animal gazing up at her with dark, soulful brown eyes was painfully homely. Her wiry coat was streaked with brown, gray, and an odd orangish color, and her head was too large for her small body. Big feet on short little legs completed the out-of-proportion picture.

"This stray is your responsibility. I found a home for the last one," Amy's neighbor Joan reminded her.

Amy groaned. They had a perpetual problem with stray animals being dumped on their rural property. Generally an advertisement in the paper would locate a new owner, but what could she say in an ad that would make someone want this pitiful mutt?

Later Amy sat toying with her pen and paper. Who wanted a homely dog? She was a lot like herself, Amy thought, ugly and alone. She had never been a raving beauty, but John had loved her. Since John passed away, this year had been a lonely one. Who wanted a 59-year-old woman who had wrinkles, gray hair, and not a single claim to beauty? She felt as if she were drifting without worth or purpose.

Amy sighed and turned again to her task. She'll just be honest, she thought. "Ugly but loving little dog," she wrote. "Free to a good home."

 Soon the phone began ringing off the hook. "Someone is already coming to look at the dog," Amy replied to the tenth caller. "I'll let you know if they decide not to take her."

A car pulled into the driveway. That's probably the Walkers, Amy thought. They must have left right after she talked to them. She went out to meet the prospective new owners with the homely little dog at her heels.

A gray-haired man slowly stepped out of the car and looked at her. "Well, she sure isn't very pretty, is she?" he asked with a smile.

"I said in the ad that she was ugly," Amy pointed out.

The dog's curly tail wagged with joy as she gazed hopefully at Mr. Walker.

"Bring her around where I can see her," a woman's voice came from the car. Amy had not noticed the woman slouched down in the passenger seat.

"My wife is not able to get out of the car easily," Mr. Walker explained. He picked up the dog and lifted her up to the passenger-side window.

The dog looked at the woman quizzically for a moment, then leaped from the man's arms into the woman's lap. With a look of adoration, she lay her head on the woman's shoulder.

Mrs. Walker hugged the dog and began crooning to her gently.

Mr. Walker grinned. "I believe we'll take her," he said.

"I can't believe the response I got from that ad," Amy said. "I didn't know there was such a market for ugly."

"It's not the ugly there's a market for," he said. "It's the loving. There's always a market for love."

Amy watched as the happy couple drove away with an ecstatic, ugly dog. Perhaps that's my trouble, she mused. Maybe she had been concentrating too much on the ugliness. Maybe she needed to concentrate more on the market for loving.

Mrs. Walker reminded Amy of a lady from her church who had recently moved to a nursing home. She would probably enjoy some homemade cookies. Then she thought of her neighbor with the fussy new baby. No doubt an afternoon off while Amy babysat would be a treat for her.

There were many things Amy could do that didn't require a pretty face, she thought.

The phone rang again. "No," she answered, "our loving little dog has already found a new home."

Dogs feel very strongly that they should always go with you in the car, in case the need should arise for them to bark violently at nothing right in your ear.

—Dave Barry

Kiki's Find

It was a dark, cloudless night, one of those nights that seem to swallow up any ambient light that might exist. It was not the greatest of conditions for a missing-person search, but it was par for the course in Kiki's and Kristie's experience.

Keahi, or "Kiki" for short, was a Belgian shepherd and Kristie's search-and-rescue dog. Kiki was the most recent search-and-rescue pup in a long line of them that Kristie had trained and worked with for almost 25 years. The two conducted nearly 50 searches a year—a strenuous pace for any search team—and they had racked up an impressive number of finds. Kiki and Kristie had led investigators to the bodies of murder victims and those who had drowned—even one found 170 feet deep in water. They had found lost children and wandering seniors on numerous occasions, and their success in doing so was a big reason why they had been called out that night.

"Are you ready to go, girl? Ready to find the little guy?" said Kristie. Kiki wagged her bushy tail as Kristie fastened the orange search-dog vest around the dog's front and clipped a leash to her collar. The two had been summoned to assist the local police in looking for a missing four-year-old boy. His mother had reported him missing about an hour before Kristie received the call, and the police had completed a thorough search of the area where they thought he might have gone based on what his mother had told them. Their search had come up unsuccessful.

"The biggest problem is that the boy has been taught not to talk to strangers," the officer in charge told Kristie during a brief phone call. "We think we might have even walked right past him at some point, but he wouldn't respond to us when we called out."

Kristie and Kiki arrived at the scene about 15 minutes after they received the call, and Kristie immediately sent Kiki to do a quick scan around the area, the first step in almost every search. Less than 20 minutes later, Kiki bounded back toward Kristie and signaled that she had found something.

Kristie asked Kiki to show her what she had found. On Kristie's command, Kiki started walking toward where she had come from and did what she had been trained to do, which is to go back and forth between Kristie and points ahead of her to direct Kristie to the boy. After a few minutes of this, Kristie lost sight of Kiki. Even her strong searchlight didn't throw light far enough to show where Kiki went. Kristie resisted the temptation to call Kiki. Instead her instincts told her to stop walking and just listen, so that's exactly what she did. The night was still and silent, but off in the distance someone was giggling. Kristie thought it sounded like a little boy's laugh.

Kristie headed toward the sound, sweeping her searchlight back and forth over the ground. Soon the light caught Kiki's tail, wagging back and forth excitedly. Kiki had located the little lost boy, and she was licking his face with her oversized, wet tongue. By the sound of things, the boy was loving every second of it.

Yes, the little boy had been taught never to speak to strangers, but no one had said anything about giggling when a happy and jubilant puppy jumped in his lap and showed him just how happy she was to have found him.

He Left the Party Alone

A Fourth of July party ended on a sad note for Alex Larson when his best friend—a mixed-breed dog named Harry—went missing. What should have been an Independence Day celebration soon turned into a search party.

Alex found Harry at the local Humane Society eight years ago, waiting for his forever home. After several years of apartment life, Alex's first order of business upon moving to a house with a yard was to get himself a dog. One look into Harry's sad eyes, and Alex knew he didn't need to look any further; he'd found "the one." And the pair had been inseparable ever since.

The two became a familiar sight in the area, driving along the country roads with Harry's head out the window and his ears flapping in the wind while Alex sang along to the radio. Harry accompanied Alex to work each day, becoming the official greeter at his owner's small insurance office. Where one went, the other followed—until the Fourth of July.

Harry was very well-behaved and certainly devoted to his owner, so it was only natural to take the pup along to the outdoor barbecue he was attending. Harry seemed to be enjoying the attention, and of course the food. The fireworks began when the sun set. The deafening booms of the holiday may have been overwhelming for Harry. He heard one especially loud bang and suddenly dashed out of the backyard. In hindsight, Alex thought that he should have known the loud noises and bright lights would spook Harry. But Alex wasn't concerned with why Harry left at this point so much as how he was going to find him.

Neighbors and friends helped Alex search for the dog throughout the evening, but the search party couldn't find a trace of him. Alex decided to spend the night at the friend's house from which Harry ran away, hoping that his dog would turn up before the night was over. Unfortunately, Harry never showed up.

The next morning Alex started making calls around town. His first call was to the closest shelter, but there was no Harry. Then he tried the police station, but they hadn't seen him either. Everyone promised to keep a lookout for the furry dog, but it didn't make Alex feel much better.

Finally, and with a heavy heart, Alex went home the following afternoon without his beloved friend.

Alex drove the long way home, hoping he might be lucky enough to find Harry. As he was pulling into his driveway, Alex spotted him. There was Harry, lying down outside the front door.

Alex speculates that the ten-mile journey may have been a hazardous one for the pup. Separated from his home by a narrow, winding river, Harry must have swum across it to return to his best friend, because not even a flowing river could stop him.

An Unexpected Meeting

Wild dogs and wolves are a common sight in the Iraqi desert. They are strays living off the land, answering to no one—and loved by no one. But when one of these dogs met an American soldier on patrol, both of their lives were changed forever.

Nubs. That's what Marine Major Brian Dennis called the mutt when he first saw him. The dog, who looked like a small German shepherd–border collie mix, stood out from the other strays by his distinctive ears. Cut off when he was a puppy—perhaps in an attempt to make him look tougher—all that was left of his ears were little nubs. The name stuck, and so did the dog.

The story began in October 2007, when Major Dennis and 11 other soldiers traveled to a military fort at the Iraq-Syria border. Nubs was among a pack of dogs hanging around the fort, where scraps were generally plentiful. When the men got out of their Humvee, Nubs came running up to Dennis and flopped on his back for a belly rub. Dennis couldn't resist.

After Dennis offered the dog part of his breakfast, he had a friend for life. Nubs began to accompany Dennis on his night patrols, walking next to the soldier as if on guard duty himself.

Over the next couple of months, the team of soldiers went back and forth between the border fort and their base. Nubs became more and more comfortable with the men, even chasing after their Humvee as they sped off each time.

In December, Dennis and his group arrived at the border fort and found Nubs badly wounded. He'd been stabbed in the side with a screwdriver. The Marines pulled out their battle kits and treated the wound, which was already infected. Whether it was the antiseptic, the antibiotics, or the TLC that Dennis and his men showered on the dog, the results were nothing short of a miracle.

That first night, Nubs was in so much pain that he refused to eat or drink and could barely lie down. The next morning, Dennis was prepared to find that his furry friend hadn't made it through the night. But he had. Once again, the men had to leave. When they came back two weeks later, they found Nubs improved—and very grateful. "I had patched him up and that seemed to be a turning point in how he viewed me," said Dennis, who was feeling the same way about his furry friend.

U.S. military personnel are not allowed to keep pets, so when Dennis and his group were assigned to a new fort 75 miles away, he had to say good-bye to Nubs, assuming he'd never see the dog again. Nubs chased after the Humvee as he had done several times before, but this time he didn't give up. Maybe he sensed that the group wouldn't be coming back. Maybe his bond was just that strong with the man who had saved him. Whatever the reason, the Humvee was soon out of sight, but the dog kept running.

For two days, Nubs trudged on. Surviving freezing temperatures, packs of wild dogs, and who knows what else, Nubs kept going in the direction that the Humvee had headed.

Dennis recalled that he was inside battalion head-quarters when a fellow Marine walked in and said, "You're not going to believe who's outside." Thinking it was a person, Dennis went outside to investigate—and there was Nubs. A bit chewed up and a little worse for wear, the dog jumped up on his friend and licked his face. Although he'd never been there before, the dog was home.

"No one really knows how he did it," says Dennis. "It was the craziest thing when he walked up. It was amazing."

So amazing, in fact, that the Marines built Nubs his own doghouse. Most of the 80 men in camp welcomed the pup, but someone complained, and Dennis was ordered to get rid of the dog.

By then, Nubs was more than just a dog to Dennis and his fellow Marines; he was a faithful companion, showing them love and a little bit of normalcy in a world far away from home. "The dog comes up to you with his tail wagging," said Dennis. "It was an escape from the drudgery, the mundane life out there, the bad things you see at times." Dennis knew he couldn't abandon the dog to an uncertain fate in Iraq, and his only other choice was to send him to America.

Unfortunately, making the decision was easier than the reality of sending Nubs back to the States. It was going to cost $5,000 to fly the dog home to San Diego. Dennis sent an e-mail to friends back home, and a Florida TV station got wind of the story. Once the story aired, it hit the Internet and the response was overwhelming. Nubs was going home to California.

From Jordan to Chicago to San Diego, Nubs arrived in the United States a month before his buddy. Dennis's friends took the dog in and began to train and socialize him. When Dennis arrived home a month later, he wasn't sure if Nubs would remember the soldier he met in Iraq— but he needn't have worried. "Nubs went crazy," he says.

Dennis found that people were so interested in the story of the miracle mutt that he worked with author Mary Nethery to write a picture book. *Nubs: The True Story of a Mutt, a Marine & a Miracle* was published in November 2009. The book is the story of how Nubs and Dennis found each other and their road home. The moral of the story? "If you're kind to someone, they'll never forget you," said Dennis. And he should know.

Scratch a dog and you'll find a permanent job.

—Franklin P. Jones

An Angel with Four Paws

The night had turned cold when Martha finally ended her shift at the restaurant. She stepped outside to head home. It had been a very busy night, with truckers coming in nonstop from the highway throughout the evening, and Martha had worked two hours of overtime to make sure everyone got what they needed. As dog-tired and aching as her feet were, she could certainly use the extra money.

She crossed the street and headed toward the tiny parking lot where she usually parked her car, but the lot was full of trucks and she couldn't spot her small car anywhere. Martha stood there for a moment, certain that the hectic shift had gotten to her brain, wondering where on earth she had parked her car. Then she remembered the lot had been full when she got there. She had parked at Lew's Deli, on the street behind the diner. She ran across the street, scolding herself for being so forgetful. She was working way too hard these days; sometimes her brain just couldn't keep up with all she had to remember.

Martha headed down the alley to the next street south, certain her vehicle would be right in front of Lew's, which was now closed. But it wasn't there. She felt a tiny ball of panic in the pit of her stomach. She took a deep breath, not wanting the panic to get any worse. Her car had to be here somewhere, unless—and she hated to even give the thought credence—it had been stolen. Just then she heard a rustling behind her. Turning, she saw a dark shadow in the alley. Panic bore down on her as she realized she was within attack distance of a huge, ominous-looking dog.

The beast had to be almost as big as she was, and Martha wasn't short. Or maybe it was just the eerie way the street lamp cast a glow on the animal, which appeared to be some kind of mutt, albeit a big and threatening one. The dog moved a step toward Martha, its fierce yellow eyes trained on her. Martha felt her throat catch as she tried to scream, to cry out for help. Nothing came out but a soft whimper. She forced her feet to move and took a wobbly step backward. The dog responded, taking another step forward, and Martha realized that she had only two choices: stay and be attacked, or run and be attacked.

Choosing the latter, Martha held her breath and ran. She rushed down another alley leading back to the diner. She didn't dare look back, but she heard the thud of the dog's heavy paws following her. She dodged between cars and trucks in the side lot, trying desperately to find her car, and she slammed right up against the cab of a pickup. It took the wind out of her for a second, long enough for her to see the dog coming out of the shadows toward her. She turned, frozen with fear, certain she was about to be attacked. She tried again to scream, to get a word out of her tight throat, but she could barely croak a whisper. "Why won't you leave me alone?" she hissed at the dog, but the animal stared at her with golden slits of eyes.

Voices off to the side of the lot caught Martha's attention. She forced her body in motion, gasping for strength, figuring that if the dog attacked her now, at least she would have some help. As she followed the noise, she found her own voice again. She was about to scream for help when she discovered the source of the voices. She had found her car, parked where she left it in a narrow alley next to the diner, but she also found two large men inside trying to hot-wire it.

As she turned to run before they could see or hear her, the two men looked up. Sensing the threat, they got out of the car and came menacingly toward her. One of them brandished a long knife, and Martha froze as the other man put his hand in his pocket and motioned as if he had a gun. She was about to beg them to take her car if they would just let her go when she heard a fierce growl behind her. In a flash of dark fury, the dog that had been following her lunged past her, landing squarely on the two men, knocking them over and attacking them. Martha screamed loudly, trying to get someone's attention. Within a minute, several truckers who had just left the diner came to her rescue.

The truckers pinned down the two bloodied and defeated car thieves as Martha ran to the diner to call the police, stopping only to look back at the dog that had clearly been following her to protect her. But the dog was nowhere in sight.

The police arrived ten minutes later to question Martha and the truckers. She told them about the dog, and when the officer did a quick check of the two suspects, the bite marks were evident. But the dog had vanished, and now the suspects would have to cope with the possibility of rabies.

As she got into her car to head home, Martha knew that her guardian angel was not rabid. As she pulled onto the main road, something made her glance over to the alley across from where the police were finishing their work. There, in the shadows, she could see two bright yellow eyes staring at her. Martha stopped her car, rolled down her window, and whispered, "Thank you." As she drove away, she knew God would send that angelic dog again, perhaps on another cold night when she had worked an extra-long shift and her feet were tired and aching.

Super Dog Performs the Heimlich

Proud dog owners often brag about their pets' feats of loyalty and even heroism, but one lucky Maryland woman has a story that takes the cake—or maybe we should say "takes the apple." She saved a dog's life by adopting him, and then he saved hers.

It all began when Debbie and her husband, Kevin, rescued a four-week-old golden retriever from a dumpster. The family already had one dog, and they weren't ready for another one. They came across a whimpering pup by accident when they stopped to investigate the noise coming from a garbage bin near their home. They knew they had to save the abandoned puppy, and that's how Toby joined the family.

Toby fit in with the brood from the start, and Debbie and Kevin settled into a happy routine with their son and two dogs. As expected, Toby had the sweet temperament associated with golden retrievers: fiercely loyal and always loving. Toby was quirky and affectionate, and Debbie would fondly call him "goofy." No one expected Toby to be named Dog of the Year by the American Society for the Prevention of Cruelty to Animals (ASPCA), but that's exactly what happened.

Toby's adventure began when Debbie, a jewelry-maker who worked from home, started to choke on a piece of apple. When she began to feel as if she couldn't breathe, she started to panic as she was home alone with only the two dogs.

Debbie remembered hearing that people can perform the Heimlich maneuver on themselves, so she tried to dislodge the piece of fruit by thrusting her abdomen against the top of a kitchen chair. When that didn't work, the panic really set in.

She started to beat her chest with her fist, and that's when Toby took action, jumping on his hind legs and using his front paws to knock Debbie to the floor. He pounced on her chest until the piece of apple popped loose. As soon as she started breathing, he licked her face as if to calm her down. Debbie says she didn't even mind the paw print–shaped bruises he left on her chest.

Several months later, Toby and his proud owners traveled to New York City's Rockefeller Center, and that's where the golden retriever collected the award of his life.

Better Together

Candice had two beloved pets. Ironically, one of them was deaf and the other was blind. But together, they were perfect.

A true animal lover, Candice has always had one or two pets ever since she was a little girl. Unlike some pet owners, she didn't consider herself a "dog person" or a "cat person." She loved them all the same.

Truman came to her first. A basset hound with long, floppy ears and soulful eyes, he was a devoted dog. In his puppy years, he was lively and playful. He adored Candice, and the feeling was mutual.

One day while watching the local news, Candice caught a segment about a stray cat that needed a home. A bit shy, the calico kitty avoided human contact until a determined cook finally captured her in the alley with the offer of leftover tuna casserole. She was turned over to the local Humane Society, where they soon discovered she was deaf.

When the little cat arrived at the shelter, she was in bad shape. Skinny with ratty fur, a host of worms, and two small cuts on her ear, they called her Tatters. They bathed her, dewormed her, and brushed her until her coat was soft and fluffy. She was ready for a forever home. The trouble was that no one seemed willing to take in a stray cat that couldn't hear.

But Candice was touched by the story. Knowing that it might be hard to find a home for Tatters, she called the Humane Society and offered to adopt the kitten.

When she first arrived at her new home, Tatters was afraid of everything. She hid under the bed for two days, eating only what was placed close enough to her that she didn't need to come out into the open.

Truman, on the other hand, was a natural with the kitten, and he welcomed the new arrival with open paws. He would inch close to the cat and calmly rest his head between his paws—the canine version of "This place is safe and calm. You'll like it here." And sure enough, Tatters did.

The two quickly became friends. With no hearing, Tatters seemed to have sharpened her other senses. Candice could tell that the kitten felt even the slightest breeze or when the floorboards vibrated and that she saw everything through eagle eyes. And Truman was always at her side and alerted her to danger.

As Truman grew older, his eyesight began to get bad, until one day he could see only shadows. Tatters seemed to realize that it was her turn to be the protector, and the deaf kitty became Truman's seeing-eye cat. She slept by his side, led him slowly to his food, and helped him navigate around the house. Together, they could do anything.

It's funny how dogs and cats know the inside of folks better than other folks do, isn't it?

—*Eleanor H. Porter*

Our Gun-Shy Mrs. Grundy

Jamie was not pleased when her husband, Rob, brought home a Chesapeake puppy, but it wasn't because the wiggly little pup enthusiastically licked her hand and every other exposed piece of skin; she did not want him raising a hunting dog. Nevertheless, Rob had high expectations of successful hunting trips and named the puppy Thor, like the god of thunder. Jamie sarcastically muttered that it was as close as he could get to "god of guns."

Thor was a rambunctious puppy, but he was easy to housebreak and eager to please. He loved fetching whatever they threw for him. Rob would throw fake birds with feathers; Jamie threw balls and chew sticks. He adored riding in the car so much that sometimes he would sit beside it and howl when it was in the driveway.

Shortly before their daughter was born, Rob went off with Thor, now full grown, for his first hunting expedition.

They returned an hour later. "Gun-shy," her husband said dejectedly. Jamie laughed so hard she went into labor.

In the glow of new parenthood, Rob's disappointment in his "hunting dog" eased. But if Thor had any confusion about his mission in life, it crystallized when Jamie first placed their daughter, Lauren, in her cradle. Thor would sit in front of the cradle whenever Lauren was in it, and he wouldn't step away until the baby fell asleep. When Lauren outgrew the cradle, Thor slept next to the crib. And when she moved to a real bed, he slept in her bedroom doorway. Thor was Lauren's faithful protector.

When Lauren was old enough to play outside, Thor's responsibilities increased. He vetted her playmates and nudged out of the yard any child he found suspicious. When play got too rough, Thor intervened with a growl but never a bite. He stayed between Lauren and the street, and when they swam in the river, he would paddle between her and the deep water. He walked her to school every morning and ran back before the dismissal bell rang so he could walk her home.

Obviously, the family's little village did not have a leash law, a fact Jamie did not mind until they sold their ugly yellow car. Somewhere in his doggy brain, Thor thought he was responsible for what they called "The Beater." The new owner lived just a few houses away from them in their cul-de-sac. He had bought the car for his son, who was about to get his driver's license.

At first Jamie and Rob attributed Thor's all-night absences to doggy hormones and a lady friend. Then they learned that he slept under The Beater every night. Thor did not seem overwhelmed by his moonlighting duties, and he continued to come home when Lauren woke up and never left until after she went to bed.

The stories going around town about Thor's obsession with The Beater seemed too fantastic to believe, and Jamie attributed Thor's reputed vigilance to small-town gossip. She was not surprised to hear that when the young man who finally got his license proudly drove off in The Beater, Thor followed. And it was not farfetched that the young man would stop and let Thor in the car. Jamie was pleased that Thor was getting so many rides in his beloved Beater, but when she heard that the dog was aggressively enforcing his idea of proper dating etiquette, she knew that their village's overactive grapevine had gone wild. Thor was just too big and too old to leap from the backseat and insert himself between a young couple who were getting too close.

Rob suggested that Jamie investigate the rumor with the young man in question, but she felt that was too nosey and, worse, too gullible.

One night, the young man knocked on their door, Thor beside him wagging his tail. The boy, dressed in a suit, explained that he was taking a young lady to a formal dance and asked if they would please keep the pup inside. And then the truth came out; he explained that he had tried to kiss a girl in the car, and Thor had thwarted every amorous attempt.

Jamie held Thor's collar tightly and wished the young man a good evening before she shut the door and collapsed in laughter. Her husband just sighed. "My dog, a gun-shy Mrs. Grundy," he said. "Thor just isn't the right name and never was." He smiled. "But Lauren will be glad to hear that she can start dating a year earlier—as long as Thor goes along for the ride."

The Shaggy Dog

Charles Shows, 86, is a retired Hollywood writer and cartoonist who worked for Walt Disney. Before succeeding in Hollywood, Charles struggled to find his niche in life. Living in Indio, California, he was desperate for work and happily accepted a job as a cop in the small desert town. "In those early days, the Indio Police Department consisted of two officers," said Charles. "The chief of police was the head of our tiny force, and I was the rest of the police force! I don't mind admitting that I am not the usual cop type. I'm too softhearted, and I can't refuse a beggar. But since I was paid to get tough when necessary, I worked hard at being a no-nonsense officer.

"The chief was also trying to act like a tough policeman. One cold winter night as I reported for duty, I got a call to investigate a problem at the Southern Pacific freight yards. The chief, who was anxious to show me how to handle police problems, decided to answer the urgent call with me. The only information we had was that some transients were trespassing by camping on railroad property."

When the two men arrived at the freight yards, they saw the tent that housed the illegal squatters. Neither officer was happy about having to throw people off Southern Pacific's property, especially in the middle of winter. "Yet, a cop is supposed to be firm with all lawbreakers, whether he likes it or not," said Charles. "So we faced the problem of arresting people who were camping in a drafty old tent. When we yelled a warning that we were the police there to arrest them, we heard no answer. Entering the makeshift shelter, we saw no bums—not a single hobo. What we did see was a pitiful little homeless family of three. Four, counting a small, shaggy puppy. A frightened, unshaven little man; a thin, sickly wife; and an undernourished boy of about ten were all just trying to survive the wintry weather."

The scared mother pulled her young boy and his puppy close to her, and the father tried to defend his home. The dead of winter is no time to arrest three poor wanderers and a dog.

Charles balked at playing the tough cop, but the chief couldn't set a bad example for his one-man force. They couldn't fail to do their job, yet they couldn't bring themselves to throw the dejected homeless family and a shivering puppy out into the empty streets on a freezing night.

The chief and Charles looked at each other and seemed to agree, without saying a word, that they had to find a way to save their jobs and not be cruel at the same time. Everyone should have a place to live. "None of us are home until all of us are home," remarked Charles.

The only thing Charles could think of was to give the wandering family a few bucks to rent a warm hotel room. But that would be breaking the law. In those days, beggars were supposed to be arrested, so giving them a gift was not an option.

"I suggested to my chief," added Charles, "that maybe we could buy the kid's puppy. That way we could legally give a few dollars to the poor travelers without breaking the law. At that point, the entire Indio Police Department—all two of us—stepped outside the hovel for a quick conference. It was agreed. We would buy the puppy and solve the dilemma."

Back in the tent, they offered the sad family a chance to avoid arrest and rent a warm room at the same time— legally. But it wasn't that easy. The policemen offered all the money they had, about $12, for the shaggy little pup. The watery-eyed mother looked at her little son and asked, "Is it okay if we sell your puppy? We could get you another dog someday." The red-eyed youngster bravely but begrudgingly agreed to the deal in order to help his family. But the look in his eyes was enough to make even a police chief cry.

It was an unhappy piece of business, but it was all they could think to do. Both men wiped their noses and gave the family the $12. Charles felt like a thief as he picked up the boy's dog, but he knew that police business was police business.

"As we walked out into the howling wind, I got an inspiration," said Charles. "I asked the chief, 'Why don't we just give the dog back?'"

"That wouldn't be real honest, son," replied the chief.

"Okay, then," Charles argued, "what if we just turned the puppy loose?"

"What good would that do?" asked his superior.

"Maybe the puppy will solve our dilemma for us."

Charles smirked as he turned the dog loose. And just as he had hoped, the loyal and shaggy puppy hightailed it straight back to his master, who was now a very happy kid.

Moon-sized smiles spread across the men's faces. They felt good about what they had done. The chief remarked, "I guess we aren't too good as cops, but at least I feel like a real human being."

"Likewise," murmured Charles as they both rushed off for a hot cup of coffee, smiling the whole way there.

Pepper's Hope

Like most ten-year-old girls, Sara adored her big brother, Pete. One day Pete came home wearing an Army uniform, and her adoration turned to awe. He was not only her protector; he was a protector of the nation. When he left for Iraq, Sara could not wait to hear about his heroism; maybe he would save a platoon or even a country.

But Pete had smaller concerns. Would Sara take care of Pepper, his Scottish terrier that was almost as old as his little sister? And Sara realized that the graying mutt only loved one person, and that person was Pete. Pepper slept in Pete's room, snuggled up to him on the sofa, and whined when he wanted to be fed or taken outside.

Sara and her mom stood at the door, waving good-bye to Pete until he turned the corner, his duffel bag slung over his shoulder. Pepper wiggled between them, his nose making a circle of fog on the glass door, his tail uncharacteristically limp and drooping.

Sara's mother sighed, "It looks like Pepper has lost his spirit," she said, "And so have I." She went to her room to cry, and Sara took Pepper for a walk to take their minds off of Pete's departure.

Pepper seemed to perk up as he sniffed every tree and made tunnels through the dead leaves with his snout. Sara kicked through the leaves, remembering walks she had taken with Pete and Pepper. Maybe Pepper was remembering, too, because his tail straightened out, and he even wagged it a few times.

In the passing weeks, Pepper treated Sara as if she were his master. He left toys in her bedroom and eventually started sleeping in bed with her, but only after he dragged Pete's pillow to her bed for him to sleep on. Caring for Pepper became part of her routine, and she sent frequent letters to Pete about how well Pepper was doing while he was away.

By Thanksgiving, Sara's mom seemed to be missing Pete more than ever. When Sara asked her questions about her brother, her answers grew more and more vague. A fog seemed to settle over their house, only briefly lifted by Pepper's enthusiasm when he heard the rattle of his food bag or saw his leash in Sara's hand.

After a small Thanksgiving dinner, Sara's mom left the dishes on the table and joined her daughter and Pepper on their walk through the woods. When they reached the table rock where Sara once threw tea parties with her dolls, the three sat down for a short rest. Sara's mom explained that Pete had been missing in action for weeks, and that the chance he would be found was diminishing. Sara's eyes started to well up, and she gripped Pepper even harder as he leaned up to lick her mother's cheek. Sara's mom smiled weakly and patted him on the head, "Pete kissed me on that very cheek when he left," she said. "You're a good dog, Pep. You have your master's empathy."

When they returned home from their walk, Sara helped her mother clean up the kitchen while Pepper followed closely behind, his nails clicking on the floor. When the house was clean, Sara's mom said she desperately needed a nap.

"But we're supposed to be decorating for Christmas," Sara said. "That's what we always do after Thanksgiving dinner."

Sara's mom insisted that she wanted to lie down on the sofa and cry, but Pepper was wagging his tail and looking at her expectantly. "Okay," she said, "we can at least hang the stockings."

Sara hung her mother's stocking then her own. Pepper ran in circles around them when he saw the little girl hang his stocking beside theirs. Sara didn't know if hanging Pete's stocking would make them feel better or worse, but she couldn't imagine the mantel without her brother's Christmas stocking. She hid a few dog treats in Pepper's stocking and some old candy canes in her mom's, but she didn't know what to put in Pete's stocking. Maybe it should just hang empty, she wondered.

It had only been an hour since their last walk, but Pepper was pacing around the living room to go out. "Again?" Sara asked. She leashed Pepper and headed to the front door, but he tugged her toward the back door. They walked outside in the chilly winter cold, and Pepper lunged to a corner of the yard and started digging.

With his tail wagging, Pepper started walking back toward the house carrying a dirt-covered bone now coated with slobber. Sara was too dispirited to struggle with him, so Pepper pranced into the house with the bone hanging out of his mouth. He ran to the mantel and dropped the bone beneath Pete's stocking. Pepper sat by the bone like a soldier guarding the crown jewels. Sara sat down and sank into the sofa, crying inside.

Sara's mom came into the room, and Sara knew she wouldn't be happy to see the disgusting bone on the hearth. Sara assumed she would throw it out immediately, but instead her mom knelt down to stroke Pepper's head and gently placed the bone in Pete's stocking. "Maybe Pepper knows something we don't," she said.

In the family's annual Christmas letter, Sara's mom wrote about how her daughter had made good grades and joined the swim team, and that she had been promoted to assistant manager at her job. With tears running down her cheeks, she wrote a paragraph about Pete. She let Sara read the letter on the computer screen. "It just sounds so hopeless, doesn't it?" her mom said.

Sara's mother pondered for a minute, then turned back to the computer, fingers flying over the keyboard. She hit print and exclaimed, "There!" She handed Sara the letter. The last paragraph was about Pete's Christmas stocking and the bone Pepper had dug up for him.

"Does that sound a bit more hopeful?" she asked. Sara nodded, and Pepper licked her ankle in agreement.

Pete opened his Christmas stocking in early January when he returned home from Iraq. He opened the presents that were waiting for him with Sara's help because his arm was in a cast. Pepper snatched his dirty bone, jumped off Pete's lap, and ran to the back door. Pete let him out without a leash and turned from the door to face his sister and mom. "Pepper's burying the bone," he said with a grin.

They Find You

Lainey and Lola had lived with their caregiver in Florida since they were pups. But these two Cavalier King Charles spaniel sisters saw their lives change suddenly at five years old when their owner passed away. Taken in by a rescue group, the pair of red-and-white dogs was placed together in a new home in Virginia. They were barely settled in when they lost that home as well, due to no fault of their own. A home willing to take both sisters was proving difficult to find. It was beginning to look like these dogs, who had been together their whole lives, might need to be separated to find them a forever home.

Meanwhile, in New Jersey, sisters Sadie and Diana were grieving the loss of two of their beloved dogs, reddish-brown and white Brittanies named Tinny and Cooper. Tinny sadly lost her battle with cancer. Barely a week later, the sisters found themselves back at the animal hospital with their boy, Cooper, who was suffering from advanced lung failure. Losing two pets so close together was heartbreaking to Sadie, Diana, and their remaining dog, Lucy.

Although they weren't yet emotionally ready, Sadie and Diana considered adopting another dog because Lucy was in a deep depression after losing her best friends. Their now lone pet refused to leave the living room at night, a time when she would normally be tucked into bed with Diana. It was the room that all three dogs had played in together their whole lives, and when left alone now— even if only for a moment—Lucy would sit in that living room howling. Sadie's and Diana's hearts were broken, and Lucy's seemed to be broken as well. A new companion for her seemed like the only solution.

The sisters took Lucy to meet several dogs, but she didn't seem to take to any of them. One dog was too bonded to her foster family; another was too intimidating for Lucy to handle. They were not having much luck locating a good "fit" for their expanding family. Their compassionate veterinarian tried to comfort them, telling them, "Tinny and Cooper were both strays that were meant to be with you. They find you."

One day while searching online again for dogs that needed adopting, preferably another Brittany, Sadie and Diana came across a website with Lainey's and Lola's picture. Even though the dogs were not Brittanies, something about these dog sisters appealed to these human sisters. Although they were red and white like Lucy, they were so small that they almost looked like they could be Lucy's puppies. Diana started exchanging e-mails with the rescue group that had the canine sisters, and soon Diana found herself heading south with her dad to meet the orphaned pair. She fell in love with the two immediately and brought them home with her that same day, praying that Lucy would accept these two new family members, too.

During the first few hours home, Lucy ignored the petite sisters. After a few hours, Sadie watched as Lucy rubbed her snout against Lola, just as she had done so many times with her old friend Tinny. Slowly, and in her own way, Lucy welcomed her new friends.

As if watching the dogs bond was not enough to ease Sadie's and Diana's grief, they found themselves constantly smiling at the two little sisters, who seemed to do little else but happily wag their tails. It took time, but gradually Sadie and Diana found themselves happy again, and Lucy no longer howled when they left the room. Lucy also went back to sleeping in Diana's bed, and during the day, she snuggled on the couch with Lainey and Lola.

"They find you," their vet had told them. They wondered if this were true. Were two spaniel sisters who lost their home destined to become family with two human sisters who had lost their dogs? Were they sent to heal their broken hearts? Whether this was the case or not, that was what Sadie and Diana believed.

Foster Dog, Forever Family

It goes without saying that people who sign up to foster rescue dogs must be animal lovers. It's the foster parent's job to help these pups adjust, nursing them back to physical and mental health while they await their new homes. It can be a very satisfying experience for a foster parent, but sometimes it's difficult to give up a dog that practically becomes a member of the family in a short period of time. This can be equally hard on the dog when it becomes attached to its new master. A foster parent is usually happy to serve as a stepping stone between the dog's past and its future, but every now and then there is one dog that tugs at a foster parent's heartstrings. Shelby was one of those dogs.

Shelby, a sweet black Lab, was brought to an animal shelter when her original owners decided that she was too much to handle. Their children were too young to take care of her, and the mother and father realized that they didn't have the time or the inclination to give her the exercise and attention she needed. They were unprepared to be dog owners.

John and Cindy were the foster parents next in line when Shelby arrived. They took her home and soon discovered that Shelby was afraid of everything: new people, new places, and loud noises. Even a gently outstretched hand made her recoil in fear. In the beginning, she hid under the bed or in a closet; the outside world was just too overwhelming.

As the days turned into weeks, John and Cindy worked with Shelby to make her feel safe and loved in their home. They would try their best to calmly coax her out from her favorite hiding places and be extra patient with her. Eventually, she began to trust them.

After a few months, Shelby would follow them everywhere and was no longer afraid to live out in the open. John and Cindy were proud of her progress, but unfortunately Shelby would become fearful once again whenever they had guests or new people in their home. They wondered if Shelby would ever be ready to move to a forever home, and they questioned whether they would be able to let her go, knowing how hard it would be for her to start over with a new family. They began to consider the possibility of adopting Shelby, but they didn't want to fall into the trap of becoming attached to every foster animal they took in. That all changed one day when Shelby was forced out of her comfort zone and showed her foster parents that love and trust could go both ways.

While John was at work on a beautiful autumn day, Cindy and Shelby went for a walk through the wooded area near their neighborhood. Shelby was leading the way when Cindy tripped on uneven ground and fell down. The dog immediately ran to Cindy's side and began to whimper, worried about her master. Cindy tried getting up, but the pain was too great, and she couldn't put any weight on her leg. She feared the worst, that it might be broken.

Shelby sat by Cindy's side, offering her comfort in the way Cindy and John had shown her. While the affection helped, comfort alone wasn't going to get Cindy the medical help she needed. She motioned to Shelby, urging the dog to go find help, but the dog was reluctant to leave her human friend. It wasn't until Cindy began to cry that Shelby seemed to realize that she had to take action.

Unfortunately, the nearest house was a quarter of a mile away. However, it was a route they took often, and Shelby remembered the way. Giving Cindy one last lick, Shelby took off. For the first time, it seemed as though Shelby wasn't thinking of her own fears but of her human companion.

When Shelby arrived at the neighbor's house, she raced to the door and started whining. She scratched at the door, pacing back and forth until someone appeared. Cheryl, who knew Shelby's story, was surprised to see the dog alone at her doorstep. When Shelby jumped up and down and began to whimper, turning in circles, Cheryl knew something was wrong. Grabbing a jacket and her cell phone, Cheryl followed the anxious dog down the path to where Cindy had fallen.

Help soon arrived, and the dog spent the afternoon with Cheryl while Cindy was in the hospital. Cindy was so thankful to her heroine Shelby. By nightfall, the foster family of three was reunited.

John and Cindy once thought that they would be forced to keep Shelby if they couldn't find a home for her, but now they knew that they could never let her go. In this case, the rescue dog became the rescuer.

Angel with an Attitude

She hated him when he first arrived. Old, grouchy, fat, and loud, Angela's new cat was not the sweet little kitten she had always wanted. Terminally ill, Angela had longed for a "buddy" to keep her company. Cancer is a lonely disease, no matter how many people love and care for you, and her sister, Annie, understood Angela's need for a feline companion. Annie's baby sister was only 28 years old, and Angela didn't have much time left. Their family wanted to accommodate her and make her feel comfortable in any way they could. If getting her a kitten would make Angela feel even a little bit better, then they were happy to provide one.

Unfortunately, the cat their mother brought home for Angela was not what she had been hoping for. Oreo had an air of independence, and he "argued" with everyone in an ornery tone. Right away Annie figured out that Angela and Oreo were kindred spirits; it just took them a little while to realize it.

Angela's new buddy wanted nothing to do with her, and she wanted nothing to do with him. "Take him back, Mom!" she ordered after a couple of days. "He hates me, and he never shuts up!"

But Oreo stayed, complaining loudly all the while. He and Angela had no choice but to get used to one another. Annie thought that when you meet someone a lot like you, you either love them or you hate them.

When Annie arrived at Angela's house each morning, Oreo was waiting at the door, and he would bolt past her the instant the door opened wide enough for him to escape. She gathered that he reciprocated Angela's feelings for him. Until the day she fell.

Her morning caregiver didn't show up that day, and Angela was so happy to have some "alone time" that she didn't call Annie or anyone else to let them know. Because her brain tumor had paralyzed her entire right side, she often fell, so they never left her by herself.

When Annie pulled up to the house, she noticed all the blinds were still shut. She immediately knew something was wrong. Running into the house, her heart racing, she rushed to Angela's room and found her unconscious, the right side of her face swollen and cut. Oreo was standing on top of her, meowing loudly at Annie as if to say, "Where have you been?" His back was arched; he was rigid and protective. If a cat can have a "worried" expression, this one had it.

Angela was never the same after that fall, and her time on earth drew to an end only a couple months later. But her guardian feline never left her side.

Whenever Annie was able to get Angela into the living room for some sunshine and a new view, Oreo followed them. As soon as Annie got her sister seated or lying down, Oreo would climb gracefully to his place of guardianship on her lap or chest. With disdain, he would glare at anyone who tried to move him, including Angela. Annie hadn't envisioned a "buddy" as committed as this one, but she had to admit, the cat had tenacity.

 As time went by and Angela became too weak to leave her bed, Oreo stayed near her at all times, leaving only for eating and brief trips outside. During Angela's last 24 hours on earth, Oreo didn't leave her once. He never ate, never went outside, never moved from his spot on Angela's chest. Somehow he knew her time was near, and he was determined to be her protector until God took his place and brought her home. Angela died surrounded by family and friends who loved her. And Oreo, the guardian angel with an attitude, was with her to the last breath.

A Pup-lifting Experience

It was the day of her mother's funeral. Christine and her husband, Stan, were running late because she was reluctant to get to the service. She didn't want to say a final good-bye.

They had come from out of town and were staying at Christine's mother's house. Several of her brothers and sisters lived nearby and had offered their homes to them, but Christine needed the quiet, and she wanted to wander with her memories through her mom's rooms. She recalled the sound of her mother's voice, her laughter, and her smile, and she focused on those treasured times, which now seemed more precious than ever.

God, help me get through this ordeal, she prayed as she wiped more tears from her eyes. She and Stan finally left the house to face the inevitable. They drove down the little lane from her mother's house to the main road that would wind around the countryside and eventually bring them into town.

Christine was so focused on her thoughts that she did not notice the strange object in the yard up ahead until they were going by it. It was moving, and that's what got her attention.

 "Stan, is that a little dog? What's the matter with him?" she asked, aroused from her gloomy thoughts. They could see that the small dog was struggling.

Stan slowed the car and said, "His head is caught in a plastic jug. Apparently someone cut the top out to make it a little larger so they could put food scraps or something in it. He probably smelled something good and forced his head in, but it was too tight to get back out. Do you think I should stop and get it off?"

"We probably have to help him," she said in concern. "Mother's neighbors have most likely left for the funeral already, so we might be his only hope. If he could have gotten himself out of that thing, he would have done so already. It will only take a minute, won't it?"

Stan stopped the car and got out. By now, other dogs from neighboring houses were running over to investigate. Since the community dogs ran freely around the country-side to hunt or forage for food, they were all acquaintances. They recognized the scared little dog by smell but seemed apprehensive of his appearance. Circling him, they yelped at the strange plastic head on their canine friend. They watched helplessly as the little dog clawed at the unyielding jug.

The little prisoner saw Stan approaching, and before Stan could get a grip on the jug, the dog raced in fear across the yard. Stan hesitated, looking at the frost on the grass, now beginning to melt in the morning sun, then looked at his dress shoes. "Do you think I should try to catch him?"

"What will he do if we don't?" Christine replied, though she was concerned about his shoes, too.

"If he runs to hide in those woods, he might starve," Stan said, thinking aloud. "Or if he continues to fight the jug, and it has a ragged edge, he might cut his throat. Dogs have a tendency to get vicious when they're hurt or afraid, even if someone is trying to help them. They'll either bite or keep running in fear."

They looked toward the scared little dog and the canine entourage that followed him, encircling him and yelping in enjoyment at this new game of cat-and-mouse. The little prisoner was running off-course, sometimes zig-zagging because he couldn't see where he was going through the jug. Finally, he stopped to fight off the jug again. Stan then tried to approach him from behind so he wouldn't be seen, but the little dog saw the shadowy blur approaching and began to run again.

Disoriented, the comical-looking streak ran in Christine's direction, evading Stan's pursuit. Christine leaped out of the car and tried to block his erratic flight by jumping in front of him and flapping her arms. In the back of her mind a warning sounded, Shoes! Shoes!, but it became a secondary concern to helping the dog.

When he got close to her and saw her dark, blurred form, the scared little animal stopped for an instant, petrified and trembling, realizing that now there were two monsterlike creatures threatening him. He wheeled around again, and the fear of Christine's sudden appearance gave him new energy to run faster than ever.

Christine ran around the pathetic-looking creature so she could direct him toward Stan. The dog wheeled around, but he was going too fast to stop in time and ran straight into Stan's arms. The entourage of dogs running alongside the little one stopped abruptly to see what would happen next.

Stan clutched the scared, struggling little dog forcefully between his knees to prevent him from biting. Then Stan twisted and pulled on the jug until it came off, carefully guarding the dog's soft throat. The little animal had lost his sense of direction. Still disoriented, he jumped off

Stan's lap and ran in a ragged course toward the homes up on the hill. Perhaps one of them was his.

When things finally settled down, Stan and Christine looked at themselves to assess the damage. They couldn't help but laugh. Both of them were panting for breath, Christine's hair was falling around her face, Stan's pant legs were dirty from holding the dog, and their shoes were wet and muddy. But they were happy and satisfied that they had accomplished the rescue.

"We don't have time to go back, but I have some paper towels under the seat, so I can wipe off our shoes as we go," Christine offered. "We can turn up the heat and maybe dry off by the time we get to the church."

They got into the car and headed toward the funeral, still smiling and feeling uplifted. It seemed odd that they had encountered such a situation until Christine real-ized that God must have orchestrated the whole thing. He knew that her spirits needed a lift in the middle of a horrible time of grief, so allowing them to help that silly dog was a wonderful way to give them a few moments of much-needed laughter and peace.

Christine smiled at Stan, then took a deep breath, knowing that she would be able to face the funeral and whatever else came their way.

Crib Mates

When Josh and Haley brought their newborn daughter, Leah, home from the hospital, they knew they would lose a lot of sleep taking care of a new baby. They also expected a few issues with their golden retriever, Andy, who, until Leah came along, was considered the king of the house. Andy owned the place, snuggling nightly with his humans, demanding their attention—and getting it—and was always very excited to see them when they returned home from work.

But now there was a new houseguest, and Andy was wary. He was allowed to go into the baby's room, but he did so with great caution, knowing that this creature was important to his humans. At first he was tentative and annoyed by the incessant crying. But once or twice Andy would sneak up to the crib where the baby lay and offer a comforting whimper. This was particularly humorous to John and Haley because the baby would actually stop crying for a moment before returning to the wild howls that no amount of rocking or nursing could quiet for very long.

Josh and Haley were exhausted, and their tempers were often short, but they made sure Andy felt wanted and offered what love and affection they could in between caring for Leah. But there were times when Andy felt left out, like when his humans sat together while Haley fed the baby, oohing and aahing over the little angel, who was quiet and content during feedings. Sometimes Andy would try to join in this family time but was almost always shooed away. So he would sit across the room and watch, looking sad and dejected, until one of his humans would walk by, scratch his head, and offer him a treat.

When Josh and Haley discovered that Leah had colic, they felt a little at ease about the constant crying, even though they were in desperate need of a decent night's sleep. At least there was a reason now, they thought. If they could only find a solution to make the baby feel better, perhaps the entire family could return to normal.

One night when Leah was especially cranky, Andy sat outside the doorway of the baby's room. He quietly entered the room and slid against the crib where the baby's hand was holding onto the side railing. He rubbed his head against the small hand, and Leah turned toward him, her eyes wide and wet with tears. Andy whimpered a quiet "hello," and the baby's crying ceased. Soon Leah's tiny fingers were running through Andy's soft fur, causing him to wag his tail in appreciation. The crying stopped long enough to send both Josh and Haley into the baby's room, wondering why she was no longer wailing.

To their surprise, Josh and Haley found Leah fast asleep, her hand still resting on Andy's head. They tried to coax Andy out of the room, but the dog refused to move away from the crib. He sat in that exact spot until he was certain the baby was asleep. Only when Leah moved her little hand from Andy's head and back into her crib, still fast asleep, did the retriever leave her side.

 Every night after that, when baby Leah would start to fuss, Andy would scamper into her room to console her, offering comfort to the little human who truly made him feel like a king.

Eventually Leah began to fall asleep on her own, and she would only cry for three reasons: to be fed, to be held, or to see her best friend and crib mate, Andy, who was always happy to oblige.

Stormy's Tree

The spring day is soft and warm, brimming with life. Savannah knows she should be filled with the giddy sense of renewal that late April has always brought her before. "Why then are cold tears running down my cheeks?" she asks herself. "Why are my fingers trembling so hard that I can scarcely hold my coffee cup while I stare out the kitchen window to the pasture beyond?" Because the grass is beginning to green under Stormy's tree.

In all the 30 years he lived with them, the sorrel-and-white spotted pony would never have allowed grass to grow under the sprawling oak at the top of the hill. Savannah can see him now, pawing intently at the soft earth until it met his satisfaction. It was his favorite spot to stand to avoid the hot summer sun, and he chose to be there during even the worst of the winter storms, ignoring the open barn.

Savannah's hands begin to steady as she loses herself in memories, remembering when Stormy came to live with them.

"He was in with a load of calves," her husband, Carl, said, after arriving home from the barn sale. He led the shaggy pony out of the trailer. "No one wanted him."

Savannah and Stormy eyed each other suspiciously.

She knew nothing about ponies, and she could tell he knew nothing about mothers. Randy and Michelle dashed out the front door and mauled the new arrival like young bear cubs. The pony's ears flickered and his eyes widened, but he accepted them calmly. Obviously, he knew a lot about kids.

"Let's name him Lightning!" Randy shouted.

"No, I want to name him Thunder!" Michelle cried insistently.

Carl grinned and winked at Savannah. "I guess we'll just have to compromise," he told them. "Let's name him, uh, Stormy."

Over the years, Savannah spent countless hours leading Stormy around the yard while giving endless rides to the children. As the years passed, they rode alone and used him for transportation—to the barn, to the pasture, and to the neighbor's. They dropped the reins on the ground and left him until they returned, if they remembered.

If they didn't, he'd come home by himself. Savannah would find him in the backyard, peacefully munching grass, his reins dragging behind him.

Often, Savannah sat on the back steps, and she and Stormy shared an apple while she told him her troubles. Somewhere behind those intelligent brown eyes, she knew he understood every word she said. He respected Carl and he loved the kids, but he and Savannah were pals.

They raised the kids together, Stormy and Savannah, and she was never sure who was doing the best job. He was more patient than she could ever be, never once objecting to whatever they did. He hauled them around with loving care until they grew so tall their feet barely cleared the ground. It wasn't long until the pony was retired to the pasture and the big oak.

Stormy was a member of the family, a part of them, and Savannah thought he'd always be there. Until one cold January day when she looked out the window and saw him lying peacefully under the oak. The winter wind ruffled his shaggy coat and gently swayed the leafless branches hanging over him, and she knew that he would not be at the gate to greet her anymore.

The memory is too fresh in her mind. She turns away from the window, spilling cold coffee on the countertop. She doesn't care. She brushes her hair back, angry that it's streaked with gray, knowing it will be grayer tomorrow. She was furious with her body for growing old, with her kids for growing up, and with Stormy for dying.

"It isn't fair," she cries silently to God, but God doesn't answer.

The trembling returns when she tries to pour another cup of coffee. When she takes a sip, she tastes salty tears running into the corners of her mouth. Her spirits lift when she hears the old truck pull into the drive. Carl has just returned from the Monday trip to the barn sale, but he doesn't come into the house, and curiosity takes her outside. The sheepish smile on his face makes her suspicious.

"She was in with a load of cattle," he tells her. "I couldn't resist."

"She" is a palomino pony, smaller than Stormy, more refined and ladylike.

Her ears pitch forward while Savannah approaches, and her heart turns over. Carl hands Savannah the lead rope and hurries into the house to phone their daughter and grandchildren.

They stare at each other for a long moment, this stranger and Savannah. Finally, Savannah leads her to the gate and turns her loose. She races across the pasture, head up, tail held like a flag. One complete circle of the fences and she slides to a stop under the oak. Savannah hears her make funny whiffing noises while she lowers her head and checks out the soft, damp earth.

In a few minutes, Savannah's daughter's car pulls into the driveway, and two blonde whirlwinds fly out and scramble across the pasture, screaming with delight. The pony's eyes are wide, but she accepts them without a fuss. She looks at Savannah with an expression that clearly asks, "Am I doing this right?"

"What's her name?" her granddaughters shout. "What's her name?"

Savannah hesitates. Is she ready to put aside the years that have gone by? Her heart aches with the pain of knowing she can never go back, but who can say that the years ahead won't be the best? She can't accept this golden pony as a replacement for the little spotted pony who's gone from her life, but perhaps this is her answer from God. Is she a symbol of the wonderful years to come?

Savannah takes a deep breath. "Sunshine," she tells them. Then she shouts out loud. "Her name is Sunshine!"

Savannah breathes in the marvelous newness of the spring day, her heart singing, and Sunshine settles down to the serious business of digging all the grass away from under the oak tree.

Cassie's Kittens

Taylor sighed as she looked around their four-room apartment. It hadn't been updated in 50 years. Gray paint crackled on top of layers of spongy wallpaper, the varnish was worn off the cabinets, and the linoleum on the kitchen floor was so badly cracked it was hard to scrub it clean. After years of being college-rental property, the apartment was so embedded with the smell of beer and cigarettes that the gallons of disinfectant she had scoured into everything still hadn't removed the odor.

Worst of all, Taylor and her husband's three youngest children and their beagle shared one bedroom. They had squeezed two sets of bunk beds into the bedroom, and they were occupied by their 15-year-old daughter, Karen, their 12-year-old son, Kendal, and their 6-year-old daughter, Cassie. Luckily, Dan, their oldest, had already moved away from home or they'd have been even more crowded. The children got some privacy by changing clothes in the bathroom, and their daughter Karen did her nightly studying at the city library. Still, none of them were coping very well with their new living situation.

Their family business had failed, leaving Taylor and her husband deeply in debt with few options. They had to sell the lovely home that they had spent the past nine years remodeling. She and her husband each had new jobs, and they knew they'd slowly climb out of their financial hole, but for now they were living in an old apartment building that they were attempting to renovate.

Taylor's deepest concern was for her daughter, Cassie. They had adopted her when she was four. Her early years had been difficult and left her traumatized. Now, just when she was beginning to feel comfortable and secure, they had moved into this ugly, crowded living space. Each member of the family was grieving their individual losses, and tempers were running short. Taylor knew Cassie didn't need this added stress.

Cassie came up with her own cure for the sadness she felt. She decided she needed a kitten to snuggle and love. She stubbornly refused to listen when Taylor tried to explain that they didn't have room for another pet. Instead, each night when she knelt to say her prayers, Cassie asked God to send her a kitten. Taylor knew that this solution was not the correct one, but she didn't know what the right solution was. So Taylor, too, prayed for an answer that would make their living conditions a little happier.

Winter approached, and the family continued to make the best of their less-than-desirable living situation. Cassie and Taylor both continued to pray—Cassie for a kitten and Taylor for an answer. One evening Taylor went out to the garage to pull some boxes of winter clothing out of storage. The box with Cassie's clothes was near the floor, and the lid had come off. Taylor could hardly believe her eyes when she saw what was in that box: A mother cat had made her bed there, and she was nursing two tiny gray kittens.

It seemed that their prayers were answered with not one kitten, but two. Cassie said it was a double blessing. Once the mama cat left her kittens and Taylor brought them inside, she was amazed at how much joy they brought to their household. The children took turns feeding and brushing them, and everyone enjoyed watching their playful antics. Even their beagle seemed happy to have them around.

Cassie had been right. Having the kittens gave them something fun to focus on, so they didn't feel as unhappy about their dreary home. While Taylor didn't see the wisdom of Cassie's idea at first, God heard and understood her pleas. He directed that mama cat to a box with Cassie's name on it so they would be certain not to miss the answers to their prayers.

Jasmine, the Surrogate Dog

It's not unusual for dogs to become surrogate mothers to another pooch's pups, but a caring greyhound named Jasmine raised the concept to new heights by nurturing animals from badger cubs to baby bunnies.

When Jasmine arrived at the Nuneaton and Warwickshire Wildlife Sanctuary in Nuneaton, England, in 2003, she was frightened, malnourished, and without hope. But the staff lavished her with love and care, and Jasmine routinely repayed that kindness by being a caring mom to almost any young animal she encountered.

Over the course of her stay at the sanctuary, Jasmine cared for 2 puppies, 4 badger cubs, 5 fox cubs, 8 guinea pigs, 15 young chickens, and 15 baby rabbits. In 2008, she even cozied up to an 11-week-old roe deer fawn that had been found almost unconscious in a field. As if by instinct, Jasmine tenderly cared for the tiny deer, protecting him from danger, snuggling with him to keep him warm, and bathing him regularly, like any mother would.

"[Jasmine] simply dotes on the animals as if they were her own; it's incredible to see," Geoff Grewcock, who runs the sanctuary, told a British newspaper. "She takes all the stress out of them and helps them to not only feel close to her but to settle into their new surroundings. As soon as an animal is brought in, she walks over, takes a sniff or two, then licks and cuddles them."

Once Jasmine took in two abandoned puppies someone had found by nearby train tracks. One pup was a Lakeland terrier mix and the other was a Jack Russell-Doberman mix. Without being told, Jasmine grabbed one puppy by the scruff of his neck as soon as she saw him and brought him to her bed, fetched the other one the same way, and then settled in to cuddle with them both. Jasmine was a natural: selfless, nurturing, and loving, no matter what breed of critter needed her love and care.

Jasmine did not have the easiest life before she was brought to the sanctuary, Grewcock notes. She was found in a garden shed near the Warwickshire police station in 2003, cowering and alone, and the officers who recovered her took the abused and neglected dog to Nuneaton. At first she was skittish and anxious around humans, but she gradually grew to love her caretakers. That love then seemed to extend to any animal at the sanctuary with which she came into contact.

"It's very touching," Grewcock observes. "Her maternal instincts take over all the time."

Jasmine passed away on October 14, 2011, but her memory and legacy live on, and she will always be remembered as the dog with an astonishing capacity for love.

A dog has the soul of a philosopher.

—*Plato*

Angel

Emma and her husband, Jim, have always felt blessed with a house full of cats. They've shared their home with 11 feline friends, all of whom were strays or from an animal shelter. And they always run an "outdoor café" on their porch to feed countless other strays. Weenie, their oldest and dearest cat, died in the fall of 1996, an especially painful time for them because Emma had recently suffered the loss of her entire family. Over a period of 11 months, her mother, father, and brother had all died of cancer. She was becoming increasingly depressed and could not bear the thought of the normally joyous holiday season without her family and Weenie.

Her downward slide became apparent at work, especially to a dear young man named Patrick. He and Emma had formed a friendship immediately after she started her job. His great sense of humor and love for laughter and practical jokes had instantly drawn her to him—he reminded her a great deal of her younger brother. Emma was also one of the few people who could see through the comedian on the outside to find the hurting teenager on the inside, crying out for attention and understanding. They were both from broken homes and had an over-whelming need to be loved. Perhaps that is what had really drawn her to him—in many ways, she understood his pain. It disturbed him to see Emma so depressed, espe-cially at Christmastime. Knowing of her great affection for cats and how much the recent loss of Weenie had added to her depression, Patrick decided to take action.

He had heard about a poor little kitten that had been left to die, but miraculously someone had heard her faint cries and rescued her. She was taken to a local veterinary clinic, where she was first fed through an eyedropper and then eventually raised on a baby bottle. She spent the first three months of her life in the clinic, receiving constant love and attention from the staff. Patrick chose the perfect "mama" for this special kitten.

On December 23, he called Emma into the kitchen at work and gave her a hand-somely wrapped package. Immediately being suspicious of a prank, she shook it. The familiar sound of a box of cat food rattled through the kitchen. Everyone who had gathered started laughing, so she went along with Patrick's joke. She ripped off the paper and was holding a box of Kitten Chow. By this time, she was laughing, too, and thanked him. "Well, at least it's something I can always use!"

At that moment, he took Emma by the hand and led her around the corner. There stood another coworker holding the most adorable little kitten she had ever seen. She was so shocked and surprised, and she couldn't believe how kind and thoughtful her young friend had been. There aren't many people who would go to such lengths to give such a meaningful gift, she thought.

Patrick looked at her and said, "I figured this was the one thing you needed to cheer you up and help you make it through this Christmas. Having a new kitten to care for will occupy your mind and bring you the happiness you deserve." Emma was laughing and crying and hugging him at the same time. For once in her life, she was speechless.

As she walked closer to the kitten, their eyes met. There was an instant connection, and Emma knew in her heart that this kitten was meant for her. The kitty scrambled into Emma's arms and crawled up the front of her Christmas cat sweatshirt until her little head was resting on Emma's right shoulder. It was there that she stayed for the rest of the afternoon, purring contently. Others tried to take her from Emma, but the feline held on to her for dear life. The kitten had adopted Emma, and she named her Angel. Everyone agreed that it was the perfect name for this tiny gift from God—and, of course, Patrick.

Emma took Angel home and introduced her to her new brothers and sisters and her stunned but pleased husband. There was no period of adjustment as there had been with the other cats. Angel walked around as though she owned the place. It seemed so familiar to her, as if she had been here before.

During Angel's first night at home, she wasn't satisfied to sleep in the cozy little bed they had carefully prepared for her downstairs. Instead, she followed Emma up the steps and took her place on her pillow. And she did the same thing every night afterward. She placed her paws around Emma's head as if holding her safely and protecting her from the world. Emma began to sleep more soundly and peacefully than she had in a very long time.

As Angel grew, they needed to change the sleeping arrangements because Emma no longer had a place on her pillow for herself. Now Angel sleeps right next to her, lengthwise with her head on the pillow, nestled close to Emma. This gives Angel close access to her owner's face when she feels the need for hugs and kisses during the night. If Emma makes the "mistake" of trying to roll over and face away from Angel, Angel is forced to get up and properly throw herself down again on the other side, letting Emma know of her displeasure at being disturbed.

Angel always seems to sense when Emma is having an especially bad day because she makes it a point to stay as close as possible to her and smother her with extra kisses. It's as if Angel gives her the strength and courage she needs to go on for another day.

Patrick is always anxious to hear of Angel's latest escapades and devilish behavior. She makes them both laugh, even more than they did before, and that is quite an accomplishment. Because of her angel, Angel, Emma is certain that she has been able to recover from her tremendous losses and once again is able to enjoy life. She was sent the best gift of all that Christmas, and Patrick was the delivery person.

Bella and Tarra

There are many "odd couples" involving dogs and other animals, but Tarra and Bella make an exceptionally unlikely duo.

For more than two decades, a Burmese elephant named Tarra toured the world as an entertainer, performing in circus acts and at amusement parks, zoos, and on television. Tarra was one of the last elephants allowed to have such a life because the importation of African elephants was halted shortly after her arrival in the United States with the passing of the African Elephant Conservation Act in 1989. At first Tarra seemed to like her life in the spotlight, but by 1995, she was ready to close down her act. She was relocated to the Elephant Sanctuary in rural Tennessee, a place for traumatized elephants to recover and roam on the nearly 3,000 acres of uninterrupted flatland.

At the sanctuary, which is licensed by the U.S. Department of Agriculture, Tarra found a new, serene life—and a new best friend.

When elephants get to the sanctuary, they usually pair up. It's typical behavior for elephants, and when they find their "friend," they spend all their time together. Most elephants find another of their kind, but Tarra found a different kind of friend: a dog named Bella.

Bella was a stray who had been taken in by the staff. Initially trained to guard a bulldozer on land purchased by the sanctuary, Bella easily fixated on big, noisy things—including elephants—if she decided that she liked them. When Bella met Tarra, there was an instant connection, and the two animals quickly became inseparable. Bella and Tarra would eat together, sleep together, run and play together, and show their affection in physical ways: Tarra would rub Bella's belly with her enormous foot—gently, of course.

When Bella suffered a spinal cord injury in 2009 and was laid up in the sanctuary office for three weeks, Tarra held vigil just outside. When Bella was carried out to the balcony to see her friend, her tail wagged incessantly. After that, the two were allowed to visit every day, and the story of their friendship made it to the CBS Evening News and then to the Internet, where the link was shared around the world, becoming an Internet classic.

In November 2011, tragedy struck this unlikely duo. Bella was believed to have been attacked by coyotes and died, leaving Tarra to mourn the loss of her friend. Sanctuary caretakers suspect Tarra found Bella's body and carried her to the spot where they often spent time together. Sanctuary workers were both heartbroken and inspired by Tarra's devotion to her canine friend despite their immense differences, and while Bella is no longer scampering around the sanctuary accompanying her elephant companion, their story continues to warm the hearts of everyone who hears it.

They [dogs] are better than human beings because they know but do not tell.

—Emily Dickinson

Miracle Maggie

Cynthia's beagle, Maggie, is her longtime friend. When her children were growing up, they called her the "healer dog" because when they were sick, they would cuddle up to her and she always made them feel better. When Cynthia's son was in college and he was feeling stressed, he would come home, pick up Maggie, and take her back to the fraternity house with him. She helped him get through the times when he had too much work to do.

In the middle of autumn one year, Maggie's hind leg seemed to be bothering her. Cynthia brought her to the veterinarian, who took X-rays and ran blood tests. He seemed very concerned. Maggie's leg was apparently not her major problem; the vet referred them to a veterinary oncologist who also performed some tests on the pup. The cost of the ultrasounds and other tests was quite high for her budget, but Cynthia wanted the best possible care for her canine friend. As her meager savings were depleted, she finally got the diagnosis: lymphoma. Cynthia was devastated. Her Maggie, her healer dog, her friend, had cancer.

The oncologist outlined her options. Maggie's spleen was so enlarged that the vet wanted to remove it immediately. She also prescribed a course of chemotherapy. Cynthia now had to weigh the pros and cons. Her heart wanted Maggie to live at any cost, but her head told her that Maggie was 14 years old—what right did Cynthia have to keep her alive for her own selfish reasons? She agonized for days.

Cynthia's children were convinced that Maggie might survive the chemotherapy, but they weren't sure if their mom would. She finally called the oncologist and said she wasn't coming back again. She would love Maggie and keep her comfortable for as long as she had her. She was told that without any therapy, Maggie had one to three months to live.

Each year, on the first Saturday in October, Cynthia's church celebrates the feast of St. Francis of Assisi, the patron saint of animals. On that Saturday Cynthia took the ailing Maggie to church to be blessed. She prayed to St. Francis, to St. Jude (patron saint of hopeless cases), and to God. She prayed for Maggie to be spared, and if that was not possible, she prayed for the wisdom to know when the time was right for her to let Maggie go. She did not want Maggie to suffer.

Weeks went by and Maggie seemed to be doing well. Three weeks before Christmas, Cynthia received a postcard from her veterinarian saying that Maggie was due for her shots. Cynthia called him to ask if the shots were really necessary. He explained that the reminder was computer generated and that they would not be giving her any more shots. However, since they hadn't been in for two months, he suggested that she bring Maggie in so he could check her out and perhaps let Cynthia know what to expect. She agreed.

Cynthia took Maggie to the vet's office. He examined her, and re-examined her, and examined her again. Cynthia finally asked, "What's wrong?" The confused-looking vet replied, "Nothing." She asked again and got the same reply.

Eventually he said, "That's the problem—there is nothing wrong with her. I can't find anything! What have you been doing since I last saw you?" Cynthia told him that she had been praying. He said, "There's no medical explanation for this. We have X-rays that show an enlarged liver. But I can palpate her liver and it's not enlarged. We have an ultrasound that shows a massively enlarged spleen. But I can feel her spleen and it's also not enlarged. There's just no explanation."

Cynthia replied excitedly, "I have an explanation. God knew I wasn't ready to let Maggie go yet, so he gave her back to me for a little while!"

It has been months since that doctor's visit, and Maggie seems to have a new lease on life. She runs down the sidewalk with her ears flapping and a little "kick" to her step. How long will this last? Who knows? Cynthia treasures every day with her angel, her Maggie. The familiar Bible saying goes, "Ask and you shall receive." Cynthia asked, and she received.

A dog teaches a boy fidelity, perseverance, and to turn around three times before lying down.

—Robert Benchley

Bubba Blues

As Jeff finished packing his suitcase for his business trip to Chicago, his little Chihuahua, Bubba, lay on the bed, looking up at him with sad, forlorn eyes. "I'll only be gone for two days," Jeff told him, scratching the bouncy dog on the head. But Bubba wailed and whined, and Jeff sat down and let the dog snuggle up to him for a few minutes before they left for the doggy hotel where Bubba would be staying.

Bubba didn't like the boarding facility despite the spacious dog playroom, where he could liberate his boundless energy with his fellow dogs. When Jeff dropped him off at the front desk, Bubba shook with anxiety and looked up at Jeff with his longing eyes as if to say, "Please, stay!" Jeff kissed him on the nose and left for the airport, leaving Bubba no choice but to resign himself to his fate.

The trip flew by quickly for Jeff, especially since he had successfully brokered a lucrative merger deal and was able to enjoy some downtime with his colleagues, touring the city and enjoying the Chicago dining scene. But he often thought of Bubba and wondered how his little pal was doing. At first he was resistant about getting a dog because of his busy travel schedule, but Bubba seemed to be okay with it, or so Jeff thought.

Back at the boarding facility, little Bubba was distraught, wailing and whining for his owner all hours of the day and night. One afternoon an employee named Brad took out his guitar during his lunch break, and Bubba's ears perked up as soon as he began to strum a few chords. Bubba listened, and then he began to howl in time with the music. Brad took his guitar to the area Bubba shared with two other dogs, and he continued to play his impromptu number. The other dogs were not amused by the serenade, but Bubba bounced up and down when Brad began to play again. The guitar player started to strum a bluesy riff, and soon the other employees were gathered around to listen to little Bubba the Chihuahua "sing" the blues.

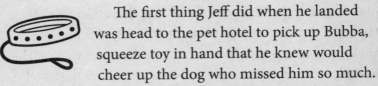
The first thing Jeff did when he landed was head to the pet hotel to pick up Bubba, squeeze toy in hand that he knew would cheer up the dog who missed him so much.
At the pickup area, Jeff smiled happily when Bubba appeared on his leash and sprinted toward his master with unabashed joy. Bubba leapt into Jeff's arms and licked his face all over as if to say, "I am so glad you're back!"

Jeff paid the bill, and the receptionist handed him a small white envelope. "What's this?" Jeff asked. She explained that they had made something special for him, and she proceeded to tell him about Bubba's newfound musical talent. In the car, Jeff opened the envelope and found a compact disc, which he popped into the dashboard player. His smile widened as the notes of a blues song filled the car, accompanied by a wail he knew well. Bubba immediately responded by howling in sync to the music, only this time the wails were joyful, not sad and dejected.

"I've got me a star," Jeff laughed, as Bubba "sang" the whole way home.

Jeff's next trip was three days long, and luckily his destination was within driving distance. He checked with the hotel and discovered that they were pet friendly, so he decided to treat Bubba to a road trip, and his canine maestro sang the blues the entire way there. On future trips, Jeff decided he will always try to take his blues aficionado along with him when he can, realizing that the best blues songs are duets. And now and then, the hotel bar has a guitarist who is happy to let little Bubba on stage to howl his heart out. Bubba is overjoyed with the attention he receives, but most of all, he loves being with his master, Jeff. And that's worth singing about.

A Moment for Paws

Kara didn't like her very much, and she certainly didn't want to adopt her. Kelly, a Shetland sheepdog mix, was a ward of the pound and in need of a good home. Kara was quite content with their family's current dog, Banner. He was a handsome, healthy purebred sheltie with beautiful coloring. Kelly, on the other hand, was an excitable, gangly, awkward young mutt. There was simply no comparison between the two, thought Kara. But Kara knew that she was not the only member of the household, and she was out-voted by her husband and daughters. Despite her protests, Kelly was moving in.

Kara had forgotten what it was like to have a young dog in the house. Kelly was full of boundless energy—she arose every day at 5:30 A.M. to bark at the birds. This was a learning experience for Kara, because until that point she thought there was only one 5:30 in a day—and it wasn't in the morning.

Even her daughters displayed disdain for Kelly once in a while. Kelly had a commando-style stealth ability to sneak into their rooms and take a stuffed animal hostage. Once in the freedom of the living room, Kelly would then remove the nose and pull out the stuffing of the beloved toy until a distraught girl happened upon the dismembering and rescued the victim. There were so many of these injuries that the girls finally opened a stuffed-animal hospital for the nose-impaired, but that didn't stop Kelly and her commando ways.

There was no doubt how Kelly had ended up in the pound. She was a runner. Every time the front door opened, she had to be held. If given the chance, Kelly would run full speed to nowhere in particular. She obviously hadn't mastered the command "come" either.

It was the first hot Sunday of the year, and Kara had been out doing chores. She came home, put away some groceries, and was tossing a load of laundry in the washer when her daughter Candice bounded into the house and down the steps.

"Can I take Banner outside for a while?" she asked.

"Sure, where are you taking her, dear?" asked Kara.

"Oh, just in the yard. Charity and I are playing there."

"Okay," Kara said as Candice grabbed Banner's leash.

Kara went back to the kitchen to finish putting away the groceries. Something felt strange: The house was oddly calm. Then she realized that Kelly wasn't in her usual position under her feet. She called Kelly's name. No reply. She started to become concerned, so she looked around the house. She checked the fenced-in backyard and still didn't see her.

Maybe Candice has her, Kara thought to herself. Going outside, she caught sight of the girls. They only had one dog. She realized Kelly must have slipped out the front door and ran away. Alarmed, Kara put on her shoes and headed for Kelly's favorite bolting place, an old abandoned railroad track.

"That silly dog," Kara sighed.

It was hot and she was wearing jeans, but Kara had to find that dog. She kept calling Kelly's name, hoping she would miraculously appear.

Minutes ticked by, and still there was no response. There were endless fields and patches of brush on either side of the tracks. Kelly could be anywhere.

Kara's heart started to sink a little as she trudged forward, focusing her thoughts on their runaway dog. She thought about how Kelly had fallen asleep by her feet the previous night and stayed perfectly still until Kara finally moved. And to her credit, Kelly was an excellent fetcher.

She would chase any ball thrown in the backyard and bring it back. This was a treat for the kids because Banner found fetching to be somewhat beneath him. He would just look at them as if to say, "You threw it, you go pick it up yourself!" It was fun watching Kelly taunt old Banner into playing. Kara chuckled out loud as she thought about how she would bounce and jump and lick Banner's ears until he'd finally concede and join in the fun. Despite her initial reservations about Kelly, she realized that she had brought a lot of joy to their household.

"Kel-ly!" Kara kept yelling.

What would the kids think if the dog was lost for good? Her children were no strangers to loss. There were many people in their lives who had come and gone, including their own birth parents. They had been Kara's adopted children for four years now, the longest time any of them had ever been in one place. They certainly did not need to grieve the disappearance of this pet. Kara whispered a silent prayer and kept on with her desperate search.

"Kel-ly, Kel-ly, where are you?" she yelled in exasperation.

It was getting extremely hot, and Kara was feeling parched. She didn't want to turn around, but she had been walking for almost an hour and had covered quite a distance. Maybe she had somehow missed Kelly along the trail, and she would come bounding out at her as she walked back home. It was hard deciding to turn around, but she did.

The walk home was difficult. By now Kara was extremely hot and thirsty, not to mention very discouraged. No dog came racing in her direction out of the bushes, and she would have to tell her family the news that Kelly was lost. Crestfallen, Kara left the abandoned tracks and started on the road toward the house.

She avoided her daughters, who were playing in the backyard, and headed down to the basement to gather up the finished load of laundry to put out on the clothesline. She would have to tell them eventually, she thought. She opened the basement door.

"Kelly!" Kara almost screamed as an exuberant and excited dog jumped all over her, barking, turning circles, and licking her face.

"You were here all this time!" Kara said, as if Kelly could understand her. "You silly thing, you must have followed me down into the laundry room. I didn't notice—I must have shut the door on you. I'm so sorry, sweetie!" Kara hugged her canine friend affectionately, happy and relieved that she found her.

Thinking that Kelly was lost helped Kara realize just how much she would miss her if she was gone. Kara thought about how easy it is for people, including herself, to overlook the precious gifts in life until we're in danger of losing them. She realized that she should appreciate and enjoy her loved ones as much as she could. Kelly definitely reminded Kara of that, and she'll never forget it.

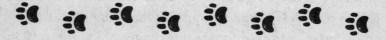

Until one has loved an animal, a part of one's soul remains unawakened.

—Anatole France

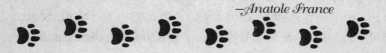